# Malta & Gozo

## by Pat Levy and Sean Sheehan

Pat Levy and Sean Sheehan have written
a number of travel guidebooks, including the
AA *Essential Turkey West Coast*, *CityPack
Hong Kong* and *CityPack Beijing*.
They are now based in London but their
home is in West Cork in Ireland.

Above: *Spinola Bay*

**AA Publishing**

7 TA GUNJU 1919

*Riots flared in 1919 when four Maltese were shot by British troops – commemorative statue, St George's Square, Valletta*

**Written by Pat Levy and Sean Sheehan**

First published 1998. Reprinted Nov 1998; Mar 1999. Second edition 2000. Reprinted Feb and Aug 2000, Feb 2001, reprinted Apr 2002. Information verified and updated. Reprinted April 2003
**This edition 2005. Information verified and updated.**
Reprinted May and Oct 2005
Reprinted Jan and Aug 2006
Reprinted Feb and July 2007

Published by AA Publishing, a trading name of Automobile Association Developments Limited, whose registered office is Fanum House, Basing View, Basingstoke, Hampshire, RG21 4EA. Registered number 1878835.

A CIP catalogue record for this book is available from the British Library.

A03510

Find out more about AA Publishing and the wide range of travel publications and services the AA provides by visiting our website at www.theAA.com/travel

Colour separation: BTB Digital Imaging Limited, Whitchurch, Hampshire
Printed and bound in Italy by Printer Trento S.r.l.

# Contents

# About this Book

## KEY TO SYMBOLS
Throughout the guide a few straightforward symbols are used to denote the following categories:

✚ map reference to the maps in the What to See section

✉ address

☎ telephone number

🕐 opening times

🍴 restaurant or café on premises or near by

Ⓜ nearest underground train station

🚌 nearest bus/tram route

🚉 nearest overground train station

⛴ nearest ferry stop

♿ facilities for visitors with disabilities

✋ admission charge

↔ other places of interest near by

❓ other practical information

▶ indicates the page where you will find a fuller description

This book is divided into five sections to cover the most important aspects of your visit to Malta and Gozo.

**Viewing Malta and Gozo** pages 5–14
An introduction to Malta and Gozo by the authors.
 Features of Malta and Gozo
 Essence of Malta and Gozo
 The Shaping of Malta and Gozo
 Peace and Quiet
 Famous of Malta and Gozo

**Top Ten** pages 15–26
The authors' choice of the Top Ten places to see in Malta and Gozo, each with practical information.

**What to See** pages 27–90
The four main areas of Malta and Gozo, each with its own brief introduction and an alphabetical listing of the main attractions.
 Practical information
 Snippets of 'Did You Know' information
 5 suggested walks
 3 suggested tours
 2 features

**Where To...** pages 91–116
The best places to eat and drink, stay, shop, take the children and be entertained.

**Practical Matters** pages 117–24
A highly visual section containing essential travel information.

**Maps**
All map references are to the individual maps found in the What to See section of this guide.
For example, the Palace of the Grand Masters in Valletta has the reference ✚ 35D4 – indicating the page on which the map is located and the grid square in which the palace is to be found. A list of the maps that have been used in this travel guide can be found in the index.

**Prices**
Where appropriate, an indication of the cost of an establishment is given by £ signs:
£££ denotes higher prices, ££ denotes average prices, while £ denotes lower charges.

**Star Ratings**
Most of the places described in this book have been given a separate rating:

😀😀😀  Do not miss
😀😀  Highly recommended
😀  Worth seeing

# Viewing
# Malta & Gozo

Above: *Marsaxlokk fisherman*
Right: *Maltese dancer*

# Authors'
# Malta & Gozo

**Mediterranean Crossroads**

If the Mediterranean Sea had a central crossroads, Malta would mark the spot. Sicily is just over 90km to the north, North Africa under 300km to the south. Spain and Gibraltar 1,820km to the west, and Egypt 1,750km to the east are roughly equidistant. Malta itself consists of two main islands, Malta and Gozo, separated by a mere 8km, with the largely uninhabited, tiny island of Comino in between.

The islands of Malta and Gozo are set right in the middle of the Mediterranean and at the narrowest point, thus smack on an ancient and turbulent crossroads. In striking contrast to their small size, their historic legacy is immense. Once the Romans came for precious honey. Today, as you gaze at honey-coloured walls, this sense of age is all enveloping. The catalogue of fearsome invaders, from ancient times to World War II, has made Malta's language, food and architecture an enticing mix of European, Arabian and British influences. Yet, unbelievably, Malta's culture is distinctively its own.

Here are prehistoric monuments built 1,000 years before the pyramids, Roman ruins and the truly awesome defensive works of the Knights of Malta, the latter largely unaltered and part of an extraordinary wealth of architecture. Agriculture and fishing are important, but this is a busy working place with good shopping, numerous markets and a buzzing tourist life.

*Painting on the prow of a luzzu is an ancient tradition that predates St Paul's arrival on Malta*

But remember: in these often over-looked islands time can come adrift. A spell may be cast by the sun and the deep turquoise sea, the scent of citrus groves on the wind, the fields of wildflowers in the spring, and the fresh Mediterranean food served alfresco with a glass of wine. Brightly painted *luzzu* (boats) bob in the harbours, and then there are the endearingly ancient cars and buses – each often carrying its own little shrine, perhaps reflecting the sometimes perilous driving conditions – red telephone boxes, and families enjoying the evening stroll or *passeggiata*. Smaller and more verdant Gozo and minute Comino enhance even further the feeling of a place apart. Once you relax into a pace of life that is full of vitality, but a few steps back in time, you may stay longer than you had intended.

Yet it is the islanders themselves one recalls with affection. They are engagingly affable: always willing to help and unfailingly polite. The Maltese are well-used to visitors but they are never cynical about tourists and a warm welcome is assured.

# Features of Malta & Gozo

## Size
Malta's longest distance from the southeast to the northwest is 27km and the widest point from east to west is 14km. Gozo is 14km long and 7km at its widest.

## Population
Some 368,000 Maltese live on the island of Malta and 30,000 live on Gozo (calling themselves Gozitans, not Maltese). Malta ranks fourth in the world in terms of population density.

## Diaspora
An estimated 300,000 Australians are of Maltese origin. Worldwide the figure is put at over 1 million.

## Government
A constitutional republic with its members of parliament elected every five years by universal suffrage.

## Languages
Maltese and English are the official languages. Italian is widely spoken, German to a lesser extent.

## Religion
Most Maltese are Roman Catholics.

## Cultural Influence
The British influence reveals itself in the colour of the telephone boxes, the popularity of afternoon tea and bacon and eggs for breakfast, and the daily use of English.

The Italian influence is evident in the popularity and prevalence of pasta and pizza dishes. Young people follow Italian trends in fashionable dress, and Italian television channels are broadcast.

The Turkish influence may still be seen in the popularity of Turkish Delight, a jelly-like, sweet dessert. The spectacular walls and bastions of Valletta may also, in one sense, be attributed to the Turks, for they were built to keep them out.

The Arab influence shows itself in the language, Maltese, 70 per cent of which is Arabic in origin.

The Catholic influence accounts for the fact that there are no divorces in Malta, abortion is illegal, and local religious festivals erupt with colour and celebration.

**Trade Links**
Malta's first application to join the European Community (now the European Union/EU) in 1990 was interrupted by the Maltese Labour Party, but the present government led Malta into the EU in May 2004. There are also important trade links with Libya and North Africa.

*Malta's first capital was the ancient town of Mdina, named by the Arabs who fortified it in the 9th century*

# Essence of Malta & Gozo

*A village festival, like this one in Qrendi, is a social occasion as much as a religious one*

Malta and Gozo draw together a richness of archaeological and architectural treasures, in an hospitable climate where the temperature climbs to 35°C and makes the clear sea the most excellent of baths and water sports a pleasure. The islands come to life with festivals known as *festas* which open up Maltese culture to visitors. Even tourist enclaves have their own festivals every night in pubs and discos. The people are Malta's strongest asset. They are proud but not narrowly nationalistic, deeply religious but not repressive, courteous but not superficial. There is an enigma somewhere but it bothers no one.

# THE **10** ESSENTIALS

*If you only have a short time to visit Malta & Gozo, or would like to get a really complete picture of the islands, here are the essentials:*

• **See the *Malta Experience*** audio-visual show (➤ 110) in Valletta for an enjoyable dip into history, covering 7,000 years in 50 minutes.

• **Go to a *festa*,** the Maltese village festival, for the fun and vitality, the colour and the sound effects (➤ 116).

• **Enjoy Maltese food** by tucking into *pastizzi* (➤ 94) with your mid-morning drink, and have at least one picnic with fresh bread bought before 11AM and peppered cheese from Gozo.

• **Spend more than a day** in Gozo because the pleasure of being there lies in its unhurried pace and a quick visit will fail to do justice to its many charms (➤ 81–90).

• **Visit St John's Co-Cathedral** in Valletta and see the Caravaggio paintings . The Italian painter came to Malta in 1607 and stayed only 14 months before he escaped from prison for an unknown crime (➤ 22).

• **See Mdina,** the ancient capital, walled by the Arabs and separated from the suburbs which became Rabat. History stares back at you from the walls (➤ 56).

• **Visit at least one of the prehistoric sites:** The Hypogeum (➤ 19) is the most informative. All bear testimony to Colin Renfrew's claim in *Before Civilization* that 'the great temples of Malta and Gozo lay claim to be the world's most impressive pre-historic monuments' (➤ 16 and 26).

• **Go for a walk around Valletta,** visiting a church here, a museum or art gallery there, forts and gardens (➤ 33).

• **Buy some Maltese glass or Maltese lace,** both artistic and affordable examples of Maltese handicrafts (➤ 105).

• **Take a cruise around the Grand Harbour,** a magnificent and truly formidable sight that sparks the imagination (➤ 110).

*Life-sized statues, carried on moveable frames, feature in religious processions*

9

# The Shaping of Malta & Gozo

**5500–4100 BC**
The Neolithic Age, when Sicilian colonists live in cave dwellings or stone and wattle-and-daub huts, use decorated red and grey pottery and create clay figurines. They farm barley, wheat and lentils, keep domesticated animals and hunt using slingstones. They import obsidian and flint from Sicily to make knives. Skorba temples are built.

**4100–2500 BC**
The 'Copper Age', when the temples at Ġgantija, Tarxien and the Hypogeum at Ħal-Safflieni are built. This highly complex society has a priest class and a religion which includes a deity, oracles and animal sacrifice as well as intricate burial rites. Potters, architects and other craft workers make delicate woven cloth and highly decorated pots. Abruptly ends around 2500 BC.

**2500–800 BC**
The Bronze Age. This culture is in many ways inferior to that of the previous era. Information about the period comes from the Tarxien Cemetery. They cremate their dead and from the grave items left in funerary urns we

*A 12th-century fresco from St Paul's and St Agatha's Catacombs*

know that they weave cloth, use copper tools, and probably have links with other cultures in the Peloponnese peninsula and southern Italy. Only a few dolmen–type structures remain. Villages are fortified, and the mysterious cart ruts at Ghar il-Kibr appear.

**c600 BC**
Comes to be dominated by the Carthaginian trading empire. Phoenician colonists trade with Greece, build temples to the Phoenician gods, strike their own coins and organise complex rock tomb burials. An inscription in both Greek and Phoenician helps decipher the Phoenician language.

**257 BC**
A Roman force invades during the Punic Wars (Romans against Carthaginians) and many settlements are totally devastated.

**218 BC**
Malta is incorporated into the Roman empire. Elaborate catacomb

burials become common. Punic temples are elaborated and Romanised villas appear in rural areas. Roman towns start to develop.

**AD 60**
St Paul, shipwrecked, converts the Roman governor to Christianity.

**AD 500–870**
Byzantine empire now in control.

**AD 870–1090**
Under Arab rule.

**1090–1530**
Colonised by succession of European powers: Normans, Germans, French and Spanish.

**1429**
Sacked by Muslims.

**1530**
Charles V of Spain gives islands in perpetuity to the Knights Hospitallers of the Order of St John of Jerusalem.

**1565**
The Great Siege. A Turkish fleet attacks the Order's settlement at Birgu, in the Grand Harbour, with the aim of taking Malta. After several months' siege relief comes from allies in Sicily.

**1566**
The city of Valletta is founded.

**1614**
A second Turkish invasion is repelled.

**1600s**
A series of forts and

towers is built around the coast, but no further Turkish invasions occur.

**1700s**
Becomes a flourishing melting pot. The Order of St John of Jerusalem declines as a fighting force, turning to trade.

**1798**
Napoleon invades. The Knights are ejected, never to return. Wholesale looting of churches. The Maltese call on the British for assistance.

**1800**
The French surrender and the British occupy the islands.

**1814**
The Treaty of Paris makes Malta a British Crown Colony.

**1835–1932**
Various attempts to establish a constitution fail.

**1914–18**
In World War I, Malta becomes 'Nurse of the Mediterranean'.

**1939**
World War II makes Malta a strategic target, bringing great hardship.

*A Maltese Knight in his armour stands to attention*

**1942**
On 15 April, the people and the island of Malta are awarded the George Cross for gallantry, by King George VI. In April alone, over 6,000 tonnes of bombs fall.

**1943**
Italy and the Allies sign an armistice on board HMS *Nelson* in Grand Harbour.

**1962**
The State of Malta is created.

**1964**
Malta achieves independence within the Commonwealth.

**1971**
The Labour Party, led by Dom Mintoff, is elected.

**1974**
Malta becomes a Republic and remains in the Commonwealth.

**1979**
British forces withdraw.

**1998**
Snap election leads to a Nationalist government. Application for EU membership is renewed.

**2004**
Malta becomes a member of the EU.

11

# Peace & Quiet

**Birdwatching**
Seabirds may be spotted from the clifftops of Gozo and the Marfa Peninsula on Malta, and the islands' strategic position as a resting station has long been appreciated by migrant species passing between northern Europe and Africa. The Ghadira Nature Reserve (☎ 347646) is worth visiting for its bird life. Admission is free and the reserve is open at weekends (closed for lunch) between November and May. Buses 44, 645 or 48 will take you there.

Coming directly from the airport to the resorts of Buġibba or St Julian's one could be forgiven for thinking there is no peace and quiet in Malta. Fortunately – because of the islands of Gozo and Comino – it is easy to correct this fallacy.

## Gozo's Appeal
Gozo may have one of the best discos and one of the best top class hotels in Malta (➤ 103), but the characteristic appeal of the place is not hedonistic. Given its small size one can cycle or walk anywhere along quiet country roads passing small family farms or following the rugged coastline along clifftop paths. Apart from the walk detailed later (➤ 87), there are several other rewarding walks and a leaflet with a map of these walks is available from the Gozo Tourist Office.

## The Blue Lagoon
The island of Comino (➤ 46) is inundated with boatloads of day visitors but it is the Blue Lagoon that is the focus of interest and, given the absence of cars and the small distances (hardly more than a kilometre in any direction), one may escape from people. It helps to be here in spring when flowers give joyful relief to the barren landscape. It is even better to stay the night, because after sunset or early in the morning you will have Comino to yourself.

*Time and the tides have combined to form the beauty of the Blue Grotto*

## Parks and Gardens

On Malta itself there are numerous opportunities to escape the hustle and bustle. The tourist office has a useful brochure listing and describing the various parks and gardens where one can seek solace, shade and enjoy a picnic far away from the fast-food restaurants and the crowds. One of the most attractive and larger parks is the San Anton Gardens

(► 44) where some of the sub-tropical trees are labelled, including a splendid pair of wide-spreading Banyan trees, *Ficus benghalensis*, on the main path, and there is a small aviary to amuse young children.

*Even the cacti blossom beautifully on the island of Gozo*

## Around Malta

Malta's capital city of Valletta is remarkably quiet and peaceful at night. Apart from a small number of restaurants and bars there is very little open after 7PM in the evening. A stroll up Triq Marsamxett to Fort St Elmo and back down the other side past the Lower Barracca Gardens is relaxing as well as offering fine views of Marsamxett Harbour and Grand Harbour (► 17).

The clifftop landscape in the southwest of Malta offers some of the best opportunities for getting away on one's own and, from April to June or September and October, this is a good place for bird watching. A recommended short walk is south from the village of Dingli (► 49) to the coast and then northwest along the ridge to Il-Qaws. With a good map one could thread one's way back to Rabat from here or return to Dingli for a bus.

---

### *Did you know ?*

*The countryside often seems barren and sun-baked but suddenly between February and May it becomes surprisingly verdant, and crocuses, tulips and fritillarias shower the fields with colour.*
*There are over 600 species of wildflowers.*
*Gozo is always greener because of its clay soil and slightly hillier landscape.*

# Famous of
# Malta & Gozo

**The Knights of Malta**
The wealth of both the Order of St John and the Knights themselves attracted artists to the island with which the Order will be for ever associated. This ensured the presence of outstanding works of art and architecture, and formidable defences.

The Knights Hospitallers of the Order of St John of Jerusalem was a religious order founded in Jerusalem in the 11th century. After the capture of Jerusalem by the Muslims in 1187, the Order moved to Rhodes, but this, too, proved temporary.

In 1530 the emperor of the Holy Roman Empire gave them the Maltese islands. The Grand Master, Jean Parisot de la Valette, made it their permanent home and prevented Suleyman from conquering Malta in the Great Siege of 1565.

The Order grouped the Knights according to language or country. Each of the eight *langues* had its own hostel or *auberge*, built around a courtyard. Five have survived.

Originally hospitallers, the Knights had become warriors, then traders and indulged in baroque architecture. Rich and dissolute living led to their decline.

For such a small island, Malta's geographical position meant that it was destined to play a memorable role in world events, notably during the centuries under the Knights of Malta and in World War II.

## Politics

Dom Mintoff (1916– ), a controversial and charismatic figure, dominated Maltese, and sometimes British, politics for 30 years. From a poor family, he attended university in Malta and won a scholarship to Oxford. He joined the post-war, pro-British Labour Party of Malta. In 1955 he became Prime Minister, proposing the full integration of Malta into the United Kingdom, but Britain refused. Mintoff immediately changed his policy to one of full independence, and resigned in 1958 to lead the Malta Liberation Movement. It was the Nationalist Party that negotiated Malta's independence. Mintoff returned to power from 1971 to 1984 and in 1996 was re-elected as a Member of Parliament.

## Art

Caravaggio (1571–1610), the greatest Italian painter of the 17th century, left his mark on the island after only a few months' stay here. He was notorious for his violent temper and, unusually, used common people as models for his paintings of the saints. Wanted for murder in Rome, he accepted a commission from the Order in 1607 and painted *The Beheading of St John the Baptist*. He became a Knight, completed three more paintings, but became involved in a fight and was expelled from the Order. He escaped from jail, and continued his short but colourful life elsewhere.

Among other famous artists to visit Malta over the centuries were the Spanish Mateo Perez d'Aleccio (1547–99), Italian Mattia Preti (1616–99) and the Frenchman Antoine de Favray (1706–98). Among the Maltese were sculptor Melchiorre Gafa (1635–67), Francesco Zahra (1710–73), Guiseppe Cali (1846–1930) and Antonio Sciortino (1879–1947).

## Architecture

Lorenzo Gafa (1630–1710), brother of Melchiorre and famed for his domes, was one of many talented architects whose monuments still stand. Gerolamo Cassar (1520–86) designed a number of Valletta's buildings, including St John's Co-Cathedral, the Grand Master's Palace and all the *auberges*. His son Vittorio (d1605), with Grand Master Wignacourt, built Forts St Lucian and St Thomas. Others included Nadrea Beli (1705–72), Antonio Ferramolio (d1550) and Francesco Laparelli da Cortona (1521–70).

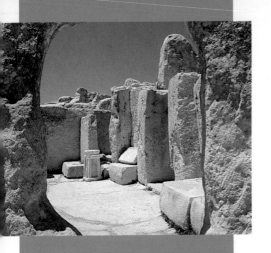

# Top Ten

Above: *Ħaġar Qim*
Right: *vessel from St Agatha's Catacombs*

15

# 1
# Ġgantija

✚ 83D3

✉ Ġgantija, near Xagħra, Gozo

☎ 21553194

◷ Daily 9–5

🍴 Oleander (££, ➤ 99) or café (£) in Xagħra (➤ 89)

🚌 64, 65 from Victoria

✋ Inexpensive

↔ Xagħra (➤ 89)

*The temples at Ġgantija arouse curiosity*

*Immense bare rock, curious features and primitive attempts at decoration are the stunning signs of a 5,000-year-old technology and culture.*

Dating back to 3500–3000 BC, Malta's 'Copper Age', the temples at Ġgantija (pronounced *Jagan-Teeya*) on Gozo are thought to be the oldest free-standing monuments in the world. The site is an artificial plateau with a sweeping panorama. Primitive in structure, it is its size which creates a sense of wonder, particularly the outer walls. According to legend, they were built by a female giant. The coralline limestone blocks which make up the outer wall, some weighing as much as 20 tonnes, were quarried from the hill on the other side of the valley and probably rolled and dragged over using the rounded stones that lie scattered around the front of the temples as rollers. The blocks were stood upright by building earth ramps, and large vertical supporting slabs support smaller rectangular blocks.

The temples themselves tell us something about the organisation and religion of the complex society that built these structures. Two buildings, one larger and older than the other, seem to have been places of worship to a fertility goddess. It has even been suggested that the

shape of the structures themselves represent the body of the goddess (head and breasts). Inside the smaller structure, about 200 years later in origin, stone female figures were found, although these belong to a later date than the construction of the buildings. In the doorway of the larger structure are hinge holes used to support doors which would once have separated the worshippers from the priests who were in the outer and central inner temples. Inside, two holes in the floor are thought to be libation holes where the blood of the sacrificed was poured. In the centre of the building, which was once 6m high with a domed roof, a large triangular stone and another one carved into the shape of a phallus were found.

# 2
# Grand Harbour

*Spread out like a living painting,
several hundred years of history bake quietly in
the Mediterranean sunshine.*

The truly formidable ramparts are best viewed from one of the many boat trips which go out into the harbour for a day or half-day trip. However, if time does not allow for that there are several good viewing points from land, particularly from Upper Barracca Gardens (▶41). Boat tours generally leave from **Sliema Marina** passing Fort Manoel on the right and crossing Marsamxett Harbour, where the northern fortifications of Valletta can be seen. Grand Harbour itself is guarded by the two forts of Fort St Elmo and Fort Ricasoli, appearing as the tour passes briefly into open sea before turning west into the harbour. As you pass Fort St Elmo damage done by the Italians in 1941 can still be seen.

✚ 29E3

**Sliema Marina**

🕐 Tours leave from Sliema Marina, check times

🍴 Lunch and dinner cruises are available

🚌 60, 61, 62, 63, 64, 67, 68 from Valletta, 70 from Buġibba, 65 from Rabat, 645 from Cirkewwa, 652 from Golden Bay

ℹ Valletta–Sliema ferry (☎ 23463333)

Built as a fortress city and developed as a naval base and dockyard by the British, Valletta sits snugly between this harbour and Marsamxett. Looking up at the towering eastern shore of Valletta the wharves of the marina, with its 16th- and 17th-century buildings, can be seen, surmounted by the Sacra Infermeria, Lower Barracca Gardens and Upper Barracca Gardens. Opposite Valletta's eastern defences are the fingers of land which make up Senglea and Vittoriosa. Between them can be seen the Cottonera Lines, a great 2-km inland defensive wall built in the 1670s. In 1565 the Knights of St John strung a chain between the tips of these two points to prevent the Turkish fleet of 200 vessels from entering Dockyard Creek, which was then the main harbour. Dominating the whole scene is Fort St Angelo (▶76).

*The grandeur of fortress-like Valletta and the Grand Harbour, seen from the air*

# 3
# Ħaġar Qim & Mnajdra

✚ 28C1

✉ 1.5km southwest of Qrendi

☎ 21424231

🕐 Daily 9–4:30 (both temples)

🍴 Bar and restaurant (££) near the car park

🚌 38, 138

♿ Few

✋ Inexpensive

*Over a thousand years before the pyramids two temples were built on an evocative and spectacular site close to the sea.*

The two temple complexes illustrate the ingenuity and complex social structure of a society that lived here for 3,000 years, then suddenly disappeared between 2500 and 1800 BC. This is megalithic architecture of a high order.

Ħaġar Qim ('Standing Stones'), first excavated in 1839, is a series of radiating oval rooms added on at various times to a trefoil structure. Holes around the entrance show where hinged doors once stood with bars to lock them shut. The stone is soft globigerina limestone which was easy to decorate, as can be seen in the pitted and spiral decoration, which accordingly has weathered badly. One stone here measures 7m by 3m.

Mnajdra, the second temple site, is a five-minute walk away in the direction of the sea but in a more sheltered spot. Made from a harder coralline limestone, it is far better preserved. The three temples share a common outer wall and presumably at one time shared a roof. There are the same patterns of pitted and spiral decorations, an outer temple with inner sanctuaries, carved recesses, trilithion door frames (two large pillars holding up a third block) and, in the second temple, an oracular window (through which the high priest or oracle might have spoken).

Both Ħaġar Qim and Mnajdra are thought to be expressions of a fertility-worshipping religion. Carved obese female figures have been found at both sites, as well as

*The megalithic architecture of Ħaġar Qim cannot fail to impress visitors*

numerous other artefacts which can be seen in the Museum of Archaeology at Valletta (▶ 39).

The small islet to be seen out at sea is Filfa, just 1km in circumference.

# 4
# Hypogeum

*This vast and complex underground carved temple with catacombs is unique in Malta and in Europe.*

This underground burial place and temple covering an area of 799sq m was discovered in 1902 by workmen, who were laying the foundations of a house when they broke through the roof of the upper temple. Realising that building would stop if the authorities discovered its existence, they kept quiet about it, but three years later the news was out. Eventually, the site was excavated and was discovered to consist of three levels of catacombs, descending to 11m, the highest and oldest level being naturally occurring chambers while the two lower levels were carved out of the soft limestone.

After a long period of renovation, the Hypogeum is once again open to the public. A visit begins with a video show that places the Hypogeum in its historical context, followed by a guided tour of the three levels. The tour provides a lot of information and questions can be asked along the way but, as the guide will tell you, there is a lot of educated conjecture when it comes to explaining the Hypogeum. The top level was in use c3000 BC as a burial ground. Descending by modern stairs to the middle level

✚ 29E2

✉ Burials Street, Paola

☎ 21825579

🕐 Daily 9–4. Tours on the hour, except noon

🍴 Cafés and restaurants in Paola (£)

🚌 8, 11

♿ None

✋ Inexpensive

❓ Tickets for the tour should be purchased in advance. Booking a week ahead can be necessary at busy times as a maximum of ten people is allowed per group.

↔ Tarxien Temples (▶ 26)

*The Hypogeum is one of the world's major archaeological sites*

the visitor encounters carved pillars as well as spiral and hexagonal decorations, probably created around 2500 BC. The guide gives a possible explanation for the Oracle Chamber and points out parts of the walls still bearing traces of the red ochre that once provided a means of decoration. Visitors can see but not step down into the lowest level.

Besides human remains, statues, amulets, vases and other objects were found during excavation. Replicas of many of these can be seen in the exhibition area at the Hypogeum; the originals are in the Museum of Archaeology in Valleta.

# 5

# National Museum of Fine Arts

🕇 34C4

✉ South Street, Valletta

☎ 21225769

🕐 Daily 9–5

🍴 The Scalini restaurant (£) opposite (➤ 93)

♿ None

✋ Inexpensive

*Enter the welcome cool and elegant interior of the building to find a minor treasure house of Western European art.*

This notable building dates back to the 16th century when it was the palace of a French Knight. Famous figures inhabiting it over the centuries included Charles d'Orleans, brother of King Louis Philippe of France, who died here. For a time it was the British Admiralty House, but was returned to Maltese ownership in 1964; it became the home of the museum in 1972. The whole style of the building, including the magnificent staircase with two flights of semicircular steps, contributes a sense of serenity and elegance to what is a noted collection of art. On three floors there are 30 rooms full of remarkable paintings. On the first floor, over a dozen rooms display paintings from the 14th to 17th centuries representing Venetian, Dutch and Italian schools. Plaster models by the local artist Sciortino are also here. Mattia Preti is well represented in rooms 12 and 13 with works such as *The Martyrdom of St Catherine*, while room 14 has paintings by Antoine de Favray and is known as Favray's Room. In room 4 are paintings by Domenico Tintoretto (a relative of the famous Tintoretto), Palma il Giovane and Andrea Vincentino.

Rooms 20 to 23 are dedicated to works by Maltese 17th- to 20th-century artists. The museum also displays a particularly fine array of antique Maltese furniture. A display of relics from the era of the Knights may reopen in the basement of the museum.

Visit to a Maltese House
*by Antoine de Favray*

# 6
# Palace of the Grand Masters

*The official residence of the Grand Masters until 1798 is now home to Malta's Parliament.*

The Palace was originally a great house built for a Grand Master's nephew in 1569. It was extended two years later by Gerolamo Cassar into a two-storey building enclosing two courtyards: Neptune Court, with its central bronze statue of Neptune, and Prince Alfred Court, each entered by a separate doorway in the rather plain façade. In Prince Alfred's Court note the Pinto Clock Tower with its mechanical figures, erected in 1745.

Inside, many of the State apartments are decorated with friezes depicting episodes from the history of the Order. There are portraits of the Grand Masters and of European monarchs, interesting furniture and works of art. In the Small Council Chamber are particularly beautiful 18th-century Gobelin tapestries. In the Hall of St Michael and St George, once the throne room, are paintings, notably a frieze showing the Great Siege by Mateo Perez d'Aleccio, a pupil of Michaelangelo. The Hall of Ambassadors is hung with red damask, paintings and another d'Aleccio frieze. The Yellow State Room, once the room where the Grand Master's retinue of pages lived, has paintings by Batoni and Ribera.

Prince Albert's Court leads to the Armoury, a converted stables, which for those with children will be the most interesting part of the visit. Here hundreds of exhibits of armour, weaponry and ordnance date back to the siege of 1565. Looking at the armour you understand why the circular steps leading up to the main building are so shallow: one suit weighed as much as 50kg, making it difficult for a knight in full armour to climb them.

35D4

Palace Square, Republic Street, Valletta

21221221

Daily 10–4

Blue Room (££–£££, ▶ 93)

Few

Inexpensive

The Palace is closed to visitors when Parliament is sitting

*An army in waiting at the Palace of the Grand Masters in Valletta*

# 7

# St John's Co-Cathedral & Museum

*Its austere, 16th-century exterior belies the stunning baroque interior, where the magnificence and wealth of the Order burgeons in works of art.*

*Prepare to be astonished when first entering St John's Co-Cathedral*

Built in the 16th century to a simple Mannerist design by Gerolamo Cassar, this was, until 1798, the Conventual Church of the Order of the Knights of St John. The wide plain façade with the two bell towers of the Co-Cathedral ('Co-' because there are two cathedrals) seems dull. Once inside though, there is almost too much to take in. It is outstanding on several levels: its historical associations, the proportions of its architecture, its rich decoration and the great diversity of its treasures. On promotion, every Knight was required to make a gift to the Order's church.

The interior, once as austere as its exterior, was redesigned in the baroque style under the supervision of Mattia Preti. A central nave has side chapels each dedicated to a different *langue* of the Order. On the barrel-vaulted ceiling is a series of oil-on-plaster paintings by Preti showing 18 episodes in the life of St John the Baptist. The striking floor is paved with the ornate and highly individual multi-coloured marble tombstones of Knights.

At the left of the main door is the Chapel of Germany, dedicated to the Epiphany. The altarpiece is 17th century by Erardi. Through the narrow ambulatory is the Chapel of Italy, which once held Caravaggio's painting *St Jerome* (now in the cathedral museum). Next, the Chapel of France, restored in the 1840s during a brief period of revulsion against baroque, has an altarpiece by Preti. The Chapel of Provence has a painting of St Michael above the altar. Beyond it is the Chapel of the Holy Relics, looted by Napoleon in 1798. Above the crypt, usually closed to the public, is the marble, lapis lazuli and bronze altar. The huge marble group in the apse by Giuseppe Mazzuoli depicts the baptism of Christ.

Across the nave is the Chapel of the Blessed Sacrament. Legend says that its silver gates were painted black to make them appear worthless during the looting by Napoleon. Inside is an icon, the *Madonna of Carafa*, presented to the Order in 1617 by a Knight.

The Chapel of Auvergne has three works by Giuseppe d'Arena, while the Chapel of Aragon contains the first piece of work done by Preti for the Knights, *St George and*

✝ 35D3

✉ St John's Square, Valletta

☎ 21225639

🕐 Mon–Fri 9:30–12:30, 1:30–4:30, Sat 9–2. Closed public holidays.

🍴 Café Marquee (£) is opposite (➤ 92)

♿ None

✋ Inexpensive

❓ Sunday High Mass at 9:15 AM in Latin and Masses in the vernacular on church festivities and days of commemoration.

*the Dragon*. Painted in 1658 in Naples, it was his sample of work aimed at obtaining the commission for the vault. Going beyond the entrance to the Oratory the last chapel is that of Castile et Léon, dedicated to St James and containing Preti's last work. Preti himself was made a Knight and his tombstone is in the sacristy.

The oratory and museum contain more wonders, including two Caravaggio paintings, *St Jerome* and *The Beheading of St John the Baptist*, the latter being his only signed work. Also on display are antiphonaries (books of chants), the surviving cathedral silver and the Flemish tapestries depicting religious stories made in the late 17th century at a huge cost. The tapestries decorate the nave during the *festa* of St John.

*The rather austere exterior of St John's Co-Cathedral, built between 1573 and 1577*

23

# 8
# St Paul's & St Agatha's Catacombs

*Wander among 3sq km of dimly lit, claustrophobic and eerily empty tombs under the ancient town of Rabat.*

56A1/B1

Triq Sant'Agata, Rabat

21454562 (St Paul's); 21454503 (St Agatha's)

Jul–Sep, Mon–Fri 9–5, Sat 9–1; Oct–Jun, Mon–Fri 9–12, 1–5, Sat 9–1. Closed Sundays and public holidays

Cafés and restaurants (£) near by

80, 81 from Valletta, 86 from Bugibba, 65 from Sliema

None

Inexpensive

St Paul's Church and Grotto (► 59)

*The crypt where St Agatha is said to have prayed while on the island in AD250. The frescoes are late 15th century, the altar is late 17th century*

St Paul's Catacombs, the largest of Rabat's catacomb complexes, is a labyrinth of corridors and burial chambers. Although plundered many years ago, the empty graves are found in three basic styles. The canopied grave is a little like a four-poster bed, with a flat slab overhung with a canopy cut from the soft limestone rock. Another type is the saddest: the *loculus*, a tiny rectangular recess cut into the wall to hold the grave of a child. Others called floor graves are cut into the floor and would have been covered with a slab of rock. A thousand corpses must once have rested here. Scattered around the graves are roughly hewn tables with circular benches around them. They were probably used by the families of the recently entombed for a religious service after the burial, or on anniversaries.

Close by, St Agatha's catacombs, below the church, are so named because the saint is said to have lived here for a while to escape the attentions of the Emperor Decius. Fewer catacombs are visited on the 30-minute tour, but there are over 30 frescoes dating back to the 12th to 15th centuries, depicting St Agatha and other Christian figures. Here is the *arcosolium* type of tomb: arched windows cut into the rock wall. In the convent beside St Agatha's Church is a museum with related and unrelated exhibits, and outside is a good green area where you can rest to recover from the gloom and low ceilings.

# 9
# St Paul's Cathedral

*An ancient cathedral that is a masterpiece in itself as well as a treasure chamber of Maltese baroque art.*

The belfries and dome – probably the finest on Malta – dominate the skyline, and the frontal exterior with three balanced bays separated by Corinthian pillars has an altogether grander presence than that of St John's Co-Cathedral in Valletta. This is the finest of Lorenzo Gafa's churches, built between 1697 and 1702. However, the interior, in the form of a Latin cross, may seem gloomy despite the profusion of reds and golds. There are numerous frescoes by Preti showing events in the life of St Paul, including the saint's appearance on a white horse when the city was besieged by Saracens in 1442. The vaulted ceiling is covered in more frescoes by Vincenzo and Antonio Manno. The carved Irish bog-oak doors to the sacristy were part of the original church which was destroyed in the earthquake of 1693. The floor is covered in the funerary slabs of church and local dignitaries. In the Chapel of the Blessed Sacrament is a 12th-century icon of the Madonna and Child. The marble font is 15th century, while the marquetry stalls date from 1481.

✚ 58C3

✉ St Paul's Square, Mdina

☎ 21454136 (cathedral); 21454697 (museum)

🕐 Mon–Sat 9–5. Sun for Mass only

🍴 Cafés and restaurants (£–££) near by (► 94–96)

🚌 80, 81, 84, 86 from Valletta, 65 from Sliema

♿ None

✋ Inexpensive

↔ Mdina and Rabat (► 56–60)

❓ Festival of Conversion of St Paul, 25 Jan. Festival of St Peter and St Paul, 29 Jun. Pontifical Masses on Church festivals. No admittance to non-devotees during church services

*The baroque beauty of the magnificent St Paul's Cathedral*

The museum stands on an ancient site, thought to be the villa of Publius, the Roman governor who was converted to Christianity by St Paul. The collection of artwork donated in 1833 includes works by Dürer and Goya, while later donations include *St John the Baptist* by Ferretti and *The Adoration of the Shepherds* by Subleyras. There are vestments of ancient lace, manuscripts and collections of silver and coins. The ground floor has a collection of Punic and Roman items, while the corridor contains the original panels from the 14th-century choir stalls of the cathedral.

# 10
# Tarxien Temples

🟥 29E2

✉ Neolithic Temples
Street, Tarxien

☎ 21695578

🕐 Daily 9–5

🍴 Nearest place for food
in the main square in
Paola, a seven-minute
walk away (£)

🚌 8, 11, 12, 13, 27, 427

♿ Good

✋ Inexpensive

↔ Hypogeum (► 19)

*The largest of the prehistoric remains was a rich
depository of art, created by temple builders, and in
striking contrast to the nearby Hypogeum.*

The oldest of the three temples in this complex is some
6,000 years old, while the other two temples were built at
later stages, presumably as additions to the original. The
South Temple, the first temple you come to, was the
second to have been built. It has a central paved square
surrounded by carved stone benches and a ritual fire was
probably lit in the centre of this area. There is a stone basin
and an altar, both used in the ceremonies that took place.
Many remains were found here, including burnt bones of
animals, which are represented on the frieze around the
next chamber's walls. The most imposing of the buildings,
the Central Temple, was the last to be built (*c*2400 BC) at
the peak of the Tarxien period. It too has a central paved
area with a hearth for sacrificial fires. One of the side
rooms contains a huge bowl carved from a single piece of
stone. These rooms were probably secret areas open only
to the priesthood. Most of these temples' doorways show
bar holes where doors or screens would have been fitted.
The third and oldest of the temples, the East Temple, has a
similar structure, although it must have been altered to
accommodate the middle building. It has the remains of a
small chamber built into the walls with a tiny hole from
which perhaps an oracle spoke. Outside are the stone balls
used to roll the huge slabs of stone into place, while
behind the temple complex are the ruins of an even earlier
building with a possible hypogeum beneath it. To the right
of the entrance gate is a stone block with cone-
shaped indentations. The small stone
balls found near by suggest
some kind of divination
machine which predicted
the future according to the
movement of the balls.
Visit the National Museum
of Archaeology in Valletta
(► 39) to see finds from
the site and an artist's
impression of what the
temples once looked like.

*Artefacts at the Tarxien
Temples point to ancient
rituals from the
prehistoric past*

# What To See

Above: *Republic Street, Valletta*
Right: *Mdina doorknocker*

27

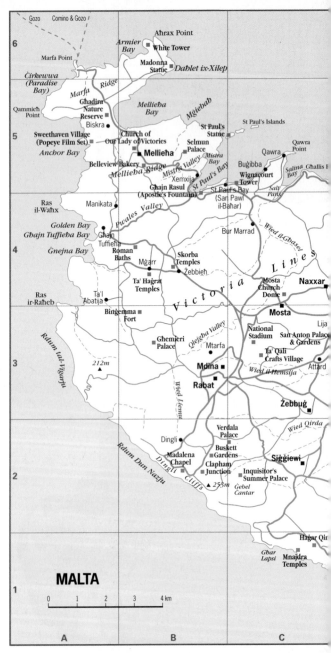

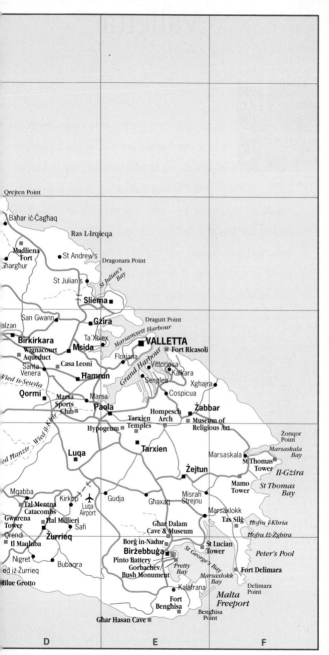

# Valletta

 All roads lead to Valletta. Nearly every bus route on the island starts and ends in the capital and anyone visiting Malta for the first time will spend some time here. The city was built after the Great Siege to create an impregnable fortress against another assault. It retains the feel of a fortified city, but is much more than a defensive town. Valletta was built as a home for the aristocratic Order of the Knights of St John, which ensured exemplary architecture, in a culturally rich Renaissance city. Despite intensive bombing during World War II, the city remains a coherent whole and visually imposing. The streets were built on a simple grid-plan but rocky terrain meant few level surfaces. The constantly shifting levels bring to mind Byron's 'cursed streets of stairs'.

> *'Adieu, ye joys of*
> *La Valette!*
> *Adieu, sirocco, sun and*
> *sweat!*
> *Adieu, thou palace rarely*
> *enter'd!*
> *Adieu, ye mansions where*
> *I've ventured!*
> *Adieu, ye cursed streets of*
> *stairs!'*

LORD BYRON
*Farewell to Malta* (1811)

# Valletta

**Francesco Laparelli da Cortona, a military engineer, arrived in Malta in 1565. His brief was to help plan a city that would permanently minimise the Turkish threat. A rocky peninsula in the north of the island was chosen as the site for a completely new city and what you see today is largely unchanged from what Laparelli planned and what his Maltese assistant, Geralamo Cassar, filled with extraordinary architecture. Valletta was the first planned city in Europe.**

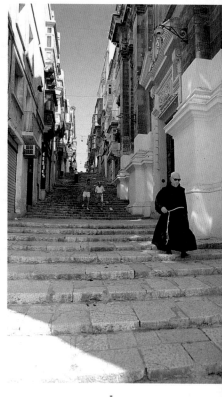

Everyone enters Valletta through the City Gate and passes directly into the pedestrianised Republic Street. It is the spine of the city that runs in a straight line for 1.5 km to Fort St Elmo at the northeast tip of the peninsula. The street passes across a number of squares, each rich in history and architecture, with bisecting side streets that lead down to one of the two enclosing harbours. Driving into Valletta is pointless because of its small size and 'streets of stairs', but this makes it ideal for walking. The city changes character during the course of the day, the best time to visit being the morning, when shops, restaurants, churches and museums are open and there is a buzz to this tiny metropolis. The afternoons are suitable for slow walks, but the streets are then devoid of people and most places are closed for an enviably long siesta. Early evening is a little more animated, especially at weekends, but the nights are strangely quiet as Valletta retreats into itself.

*Byron's 'cursed streets of stairs' are trodden by few during the afternoon hours*

35D3
Castile Square
Not open to the public
Cafés and restaurants
(£–££) within walking
distance
Good
Upper Barracca Gardens
(➤ 41)

---

35D3
Republic Square
21236585
Mon–Fri 8:15–5:45, Sat
8:15–1:15
Cafés (£–££) in Republic
Square
None
Free
Republic Square (➤ 40)

---

35E4
74 Republic Street
21231796
Mon–Sat 10–4PM. Guided
tours on the hour (last
tour 4PM)
Cafés and restaurants
(£–££) within walking
distance
Chair-bound visitors can
be helped up the stairs
and the doors on the first
floor are wide enough to
accommodate
wheelchairs
Moderate
Palace of the Grand
Masters (➤ 21)

## What to See in Valletta

### AUBERGE DE CASTILE ET LÉON

The Auberge de Castile is strategically located close to the ramparts and it is the city's most impressive example of *auberge* architecture. It dates from 1574 but the imposing baroque façade was added in the mid-18th century under Grand Master Pinto, a flamboyant bust of whom decorates the top of the stately doorway. Another admirable feature is the cornice that frames the building's roof and blends harmoniously with the louvred windows. The overall effect is that of baroque architecture at its most graceful and least complicated. The British Army had its headquarters here, and today it houses the prime minister's office.

### BIBLIOTHECA (NATIONAL LIBRARY)

This grand, late 18th-century, Venetian-style building was the last public building commissioned by the Knights. It now houses some 400,000 works, many rare or priceless, and a small selection is on display in the main hall, including the 12th-century Papal Bull instituting the Order of Knights and the 1530 Deed of Donation of Malta to the Order by Charles V. The walls of the hall are lined with books in their fine bindings. All archival material covering the history of the Knights from 1113 to 1798 is lodged in the library and it is an important source of research material for historians.

### CASA ROCCA PICCOLA

This late 16th-century dwelling was built for the Italian Knight Pietro La Rocca and is worth visiting for its period antiques. The bedroom contains a beautiful four-poster bed, the library has an intriguing wall-cabinet that functioned as a portable chapel and the various other rooms have a fascinating variety of antiques and paintings.

> ### *Did you know ?*
>
> The Order adopted the distinctive Maltese Cross
> in the mid-13th century. Each of the eight
> points symbolises one of the eight beatitudes given
> in Christ's sermon on the Mount. The points
> also represent the eight langues of the Order. The
> four main sections represent the virtues of
> Fortitude, Justice, Temperance and Prudence,
> while white denotes purity.

# A Valletta Walk

This walk begins past the Triton Fountain and through the City Gate, once the main entrance into the citadel.

*Take the first right into Ordnance Street, passing La Vittoria (▶ 38) and the Post Office next to it on the corner of Castile Square.*

The Auberge de Castile et Léon (▶ 32) is opposite, on the corner with Triq'il–Merkanti (Merchants Street). Here is a bustling scene where bargains can be found and there is a morning market.

*Walk down Merchants Street, and take the second left, signed for St John's Co-Cathedral (▶ 22–23) but return to Merchants Street for the next right turn into Triq Santa Lucia (St Lucia Street) and the St Paul's Shipwreck Church (▶ 41). Return to the Merchants Street junction but cross straight over, and turn right into Republic Street and Republic Square (▶ 40).*

It may be time for an alfresco drink or meal in the tree-lined square or a visit to the Great Siege Exhibition (▶ 38), which is tucked away next to the interior of Café Premier next to the Bibliotheca.

*Continue the walk by turning left into Triq'il–Teatru (Old Theatre Street), on the corner of the square, crossing three junctions and passing the delightful Manoel Theatre (▶ 39) before turning right into West Street. Continue down this street until reaching the sea wall where a right turn brings Fort St Elmo into view.*

Head for the fort alongside the massive city walls overlooking St Elmo Bay, taking time to contemplate the awesome defences. This walk ends at Fort St Elmo (▶ 38) at the point.

**Distance**
2km

**Time**
2-4 hours, depending on visits

**Start point**
City Gate
⊞ 34C3

**End point**
Fort St Elmo
⊞ 35F5

🛈 Tourist Information,
1 City Arcades (☎ 21237747)

**Lunch**
Eddie's (£)
✉ Republic Square
☎ 21246454

*The Italianate style of the Auberge de Castile et Léon*

33

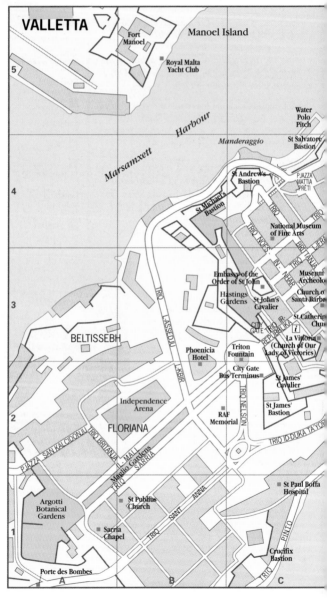

**VALLETTA**

Fort Manoel

Manoel Island

Royal Malta Yacht Club

5

Water Polo Pitch

*Harbour*

St Salvatore Bastion

*Marsamxett*

*Manderaggio*

PJAZZA MATTIA PRETI

St Andrew's Bastion

4

St Michael's Bastion

National Museum of Fine Arts

TRIQ NOFS IN NHAR

TRIQ BRITANJA

TRIQ LIFEJ

Museum Archeolo

Embassy of the Order of St John

Hastings Gardens

St John's Cavalier

Church o Santa Barba

TRIQ LASSIDJU L-KBIR

3

St Catherin Chu

CITY GATE

TRIQ IR-REPUBBLIKA

*i*

BELTISSEBH

Phoenicia Hotel

Triton Fountain

La Vittoria (Church of Our Lady of Victories)

City Gate Bus Terminus

St James' Cavalier

Independence Arena

RAF Memorial

St James' Bastion

TRIQ NELSON

2

FLORIANA

TRIQ ID-DUKA TA' YOR

PJAZZA SAN KALCIDONJU

TRIQ BRJANJA

IL-MALL

Maglio Gardens

SARRIA

TRIQ SANT' ANNA

St Paul Boffa Hospital

TRIQ PINTO

Argotti Botanical Gardens

St Publius Church

1

Sarria Chapel

Crucifix Bastion

Porte des Bombes

A          B          C

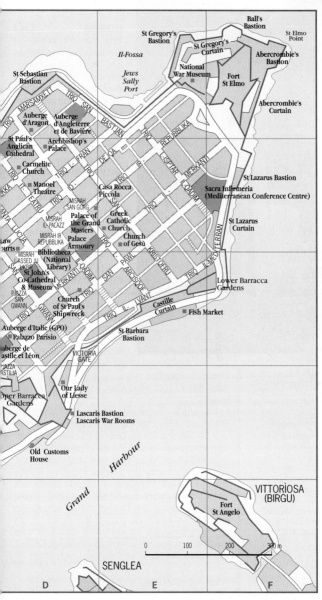

Ball's Bastion

St Gregory's Bastion

St Gregory's Curtain

St Elmo Point

Abercrombie's Bastion

Il-Fossa

National War Museum

Fort St Elmo

Jews Sally Port

St Sebastian Bastion

Abercrombie's Curtain

Auberge d'Aragon

Auberge d'Angleterre et de Bavière

TRIQ SAN BASTJAN

TRIQ

REPUBBLIKA

TRIQ

St Paul's Anglican Cathedral

Archbishop's Palace

TRIQ L-FRAN

TRIQ DEJQA

TRIQ L-ISPTAR

TRIQ MERKANTI

St Lazarus Bastion

Carmelite Church

Manoel Theatre

Casa Rocca Piccola

TRIQ L-ISPTAR

TRIQ JOADIM

Sacra Infirmeria (Mediterranean Conference Centre)

TRIQ TEATRU L-

MISRAH SAN GORG

Greek Catholic Church

TRIQ

St Lazarus Curtain

MISRAH IL-PALAZZ

Palace of the Grand Masters

Church of Gesù

MISRAH IR-REPUBBLIKA

TRIQ KRISTOFRU

SANTA LUCIJA

Law Courts

Palace Armoury

Bibliotheca (National Library)

MISRAH IL-ASSEDJU L-KBIR

TRIQ JOADIM

TRIQ SAN PAWL

TRIQ ARCISQOF

Lower Barracca Gardens

St John's Co Cathedral & Museum

MERKANTI

PIAZZA SAN GWANN

TRIQ GWANN

Church of St Paul's Shipwreck

TRIQ IL-LVANT

Castille Curtain

Fish Market

Auberge d'Italie (GPO)

Palazzo Parisio

St Barbara Bastion

Auberge de Castile et Léon

PIAZZA CASTILIA

VICTORIA GATE

Upper Barracca Gardens

Our Lady of Liesse

Lascaris Bastion
Lascaris War Rooms

Old Customs House

Grand Harbour

VITTORIOSA (BIRGU)

Fort St Angelo

SENGLEA

0    100    200    300 m

D          E          F

35

## FLORIANA ⊕⊕

This pleasant suburb of Valletta is best explored on foot (➤ 37) and although it was largely rebuilt after World War II there are some notable reminders of the past. Paolo Floriani was an Italian military engineer sent by the Pope in 1634 to further strengthen Valletta by a secondary defence system (Floriana Lines) outside the city.

The largest structure is **St Publius Church,** which was finally completed in 1792, nearly 40 years after the first stone was laid, while its classical portico is a late 19th-century addition. The entire edifice was largely rebuilt after extensive damage during World War II. The vast open space in front of the church is distinguished by a number of large stone caps which are the protruding lids to over 70 granary pits. The pits were dug in the 17th century to store food safely and they were used again from 1941 to 1943 when Malta was once more under siege.

One of the most singular churches in Malta is the circular and compact Sarria Church, built in 1676 to fulfill a vow that was made by the Order of St John at the height of a terrible plague earlier in the year. Opposite the church is the Wignacourt Water Tower, an elaborate fountain that was constructed under Grand Master Wignacourt in 1615, part of an aqueduct system built to supply Valletta with water from the hills around Mdina. The nearby Argotti Botanical Gardens, with exotic trees and rare cacti, offer an escape from the traffic that pours through Floriana. So too do Maglio Gardens, a cultured strip of garden and tree-lined walkway that stretches from the Argotti Gardens back towards Valletta.

*Above: the Grand Masters often built on a grand scale but Wignacourt Tower is a more modest edifice*

➕ 34B2

✉ To the immediate south of Valletta, a few minutes walk from the city's bus terminal

🕐 St Publius Church is open for services on Saturday evening and Sunday morning. Sarria Church has a Sunday morning service at 10:30

🍴 Cafés and restaurants (£–££) within walking distance in Valletta

♿ Good

↔ Valletta (➤ 30)

# A Walk in Floriana

To see Floriana and have an interesting, pleasing stroll, begin at the Phoenicia Hotel, on Il-Mall.

*With your back to the Phoenicia Hotel's entrance, turn right and walk down to the Independence Monument in the middle of the road. The entrance to the Maglio Gardens is immediately behind the statue. Enter the park, designed by a Grand Master as a place for young knights to exercise by playing a ball game in a large, narrow structure, since demolished. The shaded pathway is dotted with busts of various Maltese dignitaries. Over to the left the notable flat caps of the subterranean granary silos can clearly be seen in the huge square in front of St Publius Church (➤ 36).*

At the end of the park's walkway exit on the left side to view the Wignacourt Water Tower and Sarria Church on the other side of the road (➤ 36). Enter Argotti Botanical Gardens by the side of the water tower. The gardens, dating back to the late 18th century, are well-maintained and there are a number of cacti and exotic trees to admire. At the end of the walkway there is a good view from the balcony of the suburbs stretching across to Marsamxett Harbour.

*Retrace your steps to the park's entrance and cross the road to the Sarria Church. Follow the road down to the right until it meets the main road at a junction with a statue of a decrepit-looking lion gracing a fountain. Turn left and walk up the main road towards Valletta, past shops and the American Consular office, to a roundabout. Keep to the left and the Phoenicia Hotel will be seen again on the other side of the car park.*

**Distance**
2km.

**Time**
1 hour

**Start point**
Phoenicia Hotel
✚ 34B2

**End point**
Phoenicia Hotel
✚ 34B2

**Lunch**
Phoenicia Hotel (£££)
✉ Il-Mall
☎ 21225241

Part of the collection of cacti and succulent plants at the Argotti Botanical Gardens

*Right: before restoration the Manoel Theatre first served as a hostel for the homeless: later it functioned as a cinema*

### FORT ST ELMO ⭐⭐

The vulnerable tip of the Valletta peninsula was chosen by the Order of St John as the best site for their fortifications, and the fort they built was sorely tested 13 years later in 1565 when the Turks laid siege. The fort withstood the attack for 31 days. The Knights were eventually forced to surrender, but the Turks' pyrrhic victory – their losses were more than four times those of the Christians – only served to endorse the value of St Elmo, and so the fort was rebuilt and enlarged. Its star-shaped design allowed for watch towers to be strategically angled so as to guard the entrances to both harbours and the British added gun emplacements in the 19th and 20th centuries. The fort, used in the making of the film *Midnight Express*, is open to the public and is worth seeing.

**Left sidebar:**

➕ 35F5
✉ End of Republic Street and Merchants Street
☎ 21222430
🕐 Sat 1–5, Sun 9–5
🍴 Café (£) inside the fort
♿ None
🎟 Inexpensive and ticket also covers Fort St Angelo (➤ 76)
🔗 National War Museum (➤ 40), Malta Experience (➤ 110)
❓ Alarme! Historical battle re-enactment, 11AM last Sun in month, Feb–Jun, Sep–Oct (☎ 21247523)

### GREAT SIEGE OF MALTA AND THE KNIGHTS OF ST JOHN EXHIBITIONS ⭐⭐

It takes about 45 minutes to walk through the exhibition, which is brought alive using state-of-the-art technology in a graphic tableau of sound, video and 3-D environments. Collect your portable CD player (13 different languages available) and away you go at your own pace. The narrative is a little naive but the graphics are impressive and children should love it.

**Left sidebar:**

www.greatsiege.com.mt

➕ 35D4
✉ Republic Square
☎ 21247300
🕐 Mon–Sat 9–4
🍴 Cafés (£–££) in Square
🎟 Moderate
🔗 Palace of the Grand Masters (➤ 21), Bibliotheca (➤ 32)

### LA VITTORIA (CHURCH OF OUR LADY OF VICTORIES) ⭐

This church's appearance belies its historical significance, being Valletta's first place of worship when it was built in 1567 to commemorate the end of the siege, and now the oldest building in Valletta.

**Left sidebar:**

➕ 34C2
✉ Ordnance Street
🍴 Cafés and restaurants (£) within walking distance
♿ Few
🔗 Auberge de Castile et Léon (➤ 32)

### THE LASCARIS WAR ROOMS ⭐

The War Rooms were named after a French knight Jean Lascaris who became Grand Master (1636–57). The rooms were dug into the rock beneath Lascaris Bastion, and formed the subterranean headquarters of the island's defence system during the punishing bombardment of World War II. Displays, diagrams, photographs and dioramas complement the carefully refurbished command rooms.

**Left sidebar:**

➕ 35D2
✉ Upper Barracca Gardens
☎ 234936
🕐 Mon–Fri 9:30–4:30, Sat–Sun 9:30–1
🍴 Cafés and restaurants (£–££), walking distance
♿ None
🎟 Inexpensive

## MANOEL THEATRE ⭐⭐

Commissioned by the Knights of the Order of St John, this theatre opened in 1732. After a long period of disuse, then conversion to a hostel for the homeless and later a cinema, this gem of a theatre was beautifully restored in 1960. The stalls area is tiny, as is the stage, but enclosing both are three tiers of ornately decorated boxes in soft green and gold and above them a gallery area from where a spectator could reach out and touch the gilded ceiling which has a solitary chandelier in its centre. If there is an opportunity to see any performance do not hesitate to book; the theatre season runs from October to May. Regardless of performances, the courtyard café (► 53) is always worth a visit in its own right.

* 35D4
* ✉ Triq il-Teatru il-Qadim (Old Theatre Street)
* ☎ 21222618 (theatre), 21242977 (museum)
* 🕐 Guided tours Mon–Fri 10:30, 11:30, 4:30, Sat 11:30, 12:30
* 🍴 Café (£)  ♿ None
* 🎟 Inexpensive
* ↔ Palace of the Grand Masters (► 21), Bibliotheca (► 32), Republic Square (► 40), Great Siege (► 38)

## MUSEUM OF ARCHAEOLOGY ⭐⭐⭐

The Museum of Archaeology building was once the Auberge de Provence, built in 1575 and home to the most prestigious group of Knights. Although it has undergone considerable modification over the centuries, it still has its main hall where the Knights dined on iced dishes (remarkably, the ice came from Sicily). The building now houses an important collection of antiquities, and a visit is recommended as a preliminary to seeing the major prehistoric sites in Malta and Gozo. There are important sculptures from the Tarxien Temples (► 26), including the bulbous lower half of a fertility goddess that would have stood over 2m high. From Ħaġar Qim (► 18) there is a superb limestone altar and there are a number of Roman antiquities, including a huge anchor that was discovered off the northern coast in the 1960s.

* 34C3
* ✉ Republic Street
* ☎ 21221623
* 🕐 Daily 9–5
* 🍴 Cafés and restaurants (£) within walking distance
* ↔ Palace of the Grand Masters (► 21), Bibliotheca (► 32), Republic Square (► 40), Great Siege (► 38)

### NATIONAL MUSEUM OF FINE ARTS (➤ 20, TOP TEN)

### NATIONAL WAR MUSEUM ✪✪

🏛 35E5

✉ Lower St Elmo on French Curtain

☎ 21222430

🕐 Daily 9–5

🍴 Nearest café (£) is at the Sacra Infermeria

♿ Few

💷 Inexpensive

↔ Fort St Elmo (➤ 38)

❓ Lascaris War Rooms (➤ 38) are of related interest

Located under the ramparts facing Marsamxett Harbour, the vaulted hall of the War Museum is packed with

hardware, photographs and memorabilia from World War II. One of the most famous exhibits is the wingless Gladiator biplane, *Faith*, the sole survivor of the *Faith*, *Hope* and *Charity* trio of planes that formed Malta's aerial defence in 1940. Also on display is the George Cross that the people of Malta received for their heroism in 1942.

### PALACE OF THE GRAND MASTERS (➤ 21, TOP TEN)

### REPUBLIC SQUARE ✪✪

🏛 35D4

✉ Republic Square

🍴 Eddie's Café Regina (£) (➤ 92)

♿ Good

↔ All places of interest in Valletta are within walking distance

The surrounding cafés and their outdoor tables have made this centrally located square a natural meeting place and point of orientation in Valletta. It was called Queen's Square under the British, who reinforced the point by placing a statue of Queen Victoria here in 1891. The lace-clad queen now surveys the tourists who enjoy watching the world go by under the superb backdrop of the Bibliotheca.

### SACRA INFERMERIA ✪✪

🏛 35F4

✉ Mediterranean Street

☎ 21243840

🕐 Mon–Fri 9:30–4:30, Sat–Sun 9:30–4

🍴 Café (£) on the premises

💷 Inexpensive

↔ Fort St Elmo and National War Museum (➤ 38 and above)

❓ Conducted tours

The Order of St John may have degenerated into an aristocrat's club but it began life as an association of noble hospitallers, so not surprisingly the Holy Infirmary (Sacra Infermeria) was one of Valletta's early buildings, receiving its first patients in 1574. It soon became famous for its high standards, as well as its grand interior. The Great Ward, 153m long, has one of the longest unsupported roof expanses in Europe. During World War II it was seriously damaged through bombing and after extensive renovation it reopened as the Mediterranean Conference Centre. See the excellent Malta Experience (➤ 110) audio-visual film show here in a modern auditorium.

### ST JOHN'S CO-CATHEDRAL AND MUSEUM (➤ 22–23, TOP TEN)

*The Maltese suffered stoically in World War II and the award of the George Cross paid tribute to their endurance*

## ST PAUL'S SHIPWRECK CHURCH ✪✪

Originally designed by Gerolamo Cassar in the 16th century, the church underwent extensive modifications and gained a number of adornments that are now its chief attractions. These include ceiling frescoes, an altarpiece by the Florentine artist Paladini, and a piece of St Paul's wristbone behind a glass case on an altar. Another altar contains part of the block on which St Paul is said to have been beheaded in Rome, to be seen indistinctly from a distance. The statue of St Paul, by Melchiorre Gaffa, is carried through the streets on 10 February, the day St Paul's shipwreck is commemorated.

🕆 35D3
⊠ Triq San Pawl (St Paul's Street)
☎ 21223348
🕐 Daily 9–7, except during Mass
🍴 Cafés and restaurants (£) within walking distance
♿ None
💷 Free
↔ Bibliotheca (➤ 32), Republic Square (➤ 40)

## TRADITIONS AND CRAFTS OF MALTA ✪

Animated life-size figures and artefacts from the past help re-create what local rural life was like on the islands around a hundred years ago. There is little of the high-tech wizardry that characterises so many of the other exhibitions around Malta and it is none the worse for this; on the contrary, this is an eloquent tetsimony to the lifestyle of those who toiled on the land as opposed to the war games of knights. There is a delightful shady beer garden and a small gift shop.

🕆 34C3
⊠ St John Cavalier Street
☎ 21240292
🕐 Daily 9:30–5
🍴 Café (£) on premises; St James Cavalier Centre for Creativity (➤ 110)
💷 Inexpensive
↔ St James Cavalier Centre for Creativity (➤ 110)

## UPPER BARRACCA GARDENS ✪✪

These 18th-century gardens on top of St Peter and St Paul's demi-bastion were planned as a roofed playground for Italian knights but the arches are the only reminder that the place was once covered. Now open to the air, the gardens offer excellent views of the Grand Harbour and Vittoriosa across the water and they also provide one of the best places for a picnic in Valletta. The gardens are dotted with statues, the most interesting being Sciortino's *Les Gavroches*.

🕆 35D2
⊠ Castile Place
🍴 Cafés and restaurants (£) within walking distance
♿ Few
↔ Auberge de Castile et Léon (➤ 32)

### *Did you know ?*

*Malta was the most heavily and most consistently bombed target in World War II. The people and the island were awarded the George Cross for 'Heroism and a Devotion that will long be famous in History'. The medal in the War Museum is said to be the original but rumour has it that the real medal is under lock and key elsewhere.*

# Around Malta

This small island has a deceptively large number of places worth seeing, so much so that visitors need to make choices about where to go and what to see. If sea, sand and a lively nightlife is a priority then head for St Julian's, Buġibba or Paceville on the north coast. A plethora of tourist hotels and restaurants cater to an annual invasion of those seeking entertainment, a Mediterranean ambience and a suntan. On a smaller scale is the fishing village of Marsaskala on the eastern side. One can travel around easily and visitors seeking a sense of the past should visit the ancient capital of Mdina, for few places in Europe evoke the medieval era so effortlessly.

*'For there is every variety of luxury, animal, mineral and vegetable – a Bishop and daughter, pease and artichokes, works in marble and fillagree, red mullet, and Archdeacon, Mandarin Oranges, Admirals and Generals, Marsala Wine 10d a bottle – religious processions, poodles, geraniums, balls, bacon, baboons, books and what not.'*

EDWARD LEAR
Letter to Lady Waldegrave (13 February 1866)

———————————●———————————

## What to See Around Malta

### ATTARD ⊕⊕

28C3

✉ 7km southwest of Valletta

🍴 Corinthia Palace Hotel (££–£££)

🚌 40, 80, 81, 84, 810

♿ Good

↔ Balzan & Lija (see below)

*Visitors are allowed closer access to the president's residence than would be the case in most European countries*

Attard and the neighbouring villages of Balzan and Lija (see below) are known collectively as the Three Villages, but it is Attard that has the chief claim to fame. Historically, it is associated with the 17th-century Grand Master Antoine de Paule, a hedonist who is infamously linked with the decline of the Order of St John into decadence. His summer residence near Attard, San Anton Palace, is now the official residence of Malta's president.

Although its interior cannot be visited, the San Anton Gardens are open to the public. In Attard itself the Church St Mary is a splendid example of Renaissance church architecture, designed by Tommaso Dingli when he was only 22 years old.

### BALZAN AND LIJA ⊕

Balzan 29D3, Lija 28C3

✉ 7km southwest of Valletta

🍴 Corinthia Room (£££, ► 93)

🚌 40

♿ None

↔ Attard (see above)

These two adjoining villages, just a short walk north of Attard, are of interest principally because of their churches. In Balzan the Church of the Annunciation and the Church of St Roque, dating back to the late 16th century, are both well preserved. Lija's Church of St Saviour looks uninspiring from the outside, but on a Sunday morning the late 17th-century painted interior can be appreciated. A 10-minute walk away in St Saviour Street is the Tal-Mirakli Church (Our Lady of Miracles), said to be sited in the exact geographical centre of Malta. It was rebuilt in the 17th century and has a fine altarpiece by Mattia Preti.

### BIRKIRKARA ✪

Visitors tend to just drive through the urban sprawl of Birkirkara and indeed from the window of a vehicle it does not seem very inviting. Among the numerous churches is the Collegiate Church of St Helen, the largest on Malta and a notable example of ecclesiastical baroque architecture. The exterior has a striking façade and entablature while inside are some beautiful and graceful frescoes. In the older part of town there is still a lot of character in the confusing maze of streets and houses.

🕂 29D3
✉ 6km southwest of Valletta
🍴 Better to eat in Attard or Lija
🚌 42–45, 50 (summer only), 52 (mornings only), 71
♿ Few
↔ Attard, Balzan and Lija

### BIRŻEBBUĠA ✪✪

Despite the seaside setting, Birżebbuġa is not recommended as a resort – the water is sometimes polluted – but its prehistoric cliff cave of Għar Dalam and museum are well worth seeing. The cave was first inhabited by stone age humans around 4000 BC (the last occupants were evicted in 1911) but excavations have revealed animal bones that go back some quarter of a million years: dwarf elephants, bears and hippopotamuses. More remains of animals have been found that may have lived within a cave only 145m long; the cave somehow functioned as a natural trap for animals.

🕂 29E1
✉ 10km southeast of Valletta. Għar Dalam is 1km north of Birżebbuġa
🕐 Daily 9–5
🍴 Restaurant (£–££) at the Sea Breeze hotel in nearby Pretty Bay
🚌 11–13, 15
♿ None
💷 Inexpensive
↔ Marsaxlokk (► 55)

### BLUE GROTTO ✪✪

The Blue Grotto experience is a half-hour trip along the coast by colourfully painted boat from Wied-iż-Żurrieq, passing through a series of natural sea caves with picturesque rock formations. Its popularity with tour coaches can mean waiting in a queue, so try to arrive early in the morning.

🕂 29D1
✉ Wied-iż-Żurrieq, 3km southwest of Żurrieq
☎ 21640058
🕐 Daily 8–4
🍴 Cafés (£) between the car park and the sea
🚌 38, 138
♿ None
💷 Inexpensive
↔ Ħaġar Qim & Mnajdra (► 18), Qrendi (► 64), Żurrieq (► 79)

*The beautiful Blue Grotto*

28B2

4km south of Rabat

Light refreshments available but a picnic is recommended

81   Few

Free

Clapham Junction (see below), Dingli Cliffs (➤ 49), Verdala Palace (➤ 73)

---

28B2

0.5km south of Buskett Gardens

81

None

Free

Buskett Gardens (see above), Dingli Cliffs (➤ 49), Verdala Palace (➤ 73)

---

83F2

Comino Hotel (££)

From Malta and Gozo

None

## BUĠIBBA (➤ 63, QAWRA AND BUĠIBBA)

### BUSKETT GARDENS

These woodland gardens were created under Grand Master Lascaris in the 17th century with the practical purpose of raising hunting falcons. Today they offer welcoming shade during the heat of the summer. The name is taken from *boschetto* ('little wood') and the gardens reveal a botanically diverse collection of trees, including pine and oak as well as groves of oranges and olives. It is the perfect place to picnic and many Maltese families do just that at weekends. It is the only woodland area on the island.

### CLAPHAM JUNCTION

This network of cart ruts, parallel grooves cut into the rock that sometimes cross each other like railway lines, was named by the British after a busy London rail interchange. It is generally thought that Bronze Age (2000–1000 BC) people made them with some kind of non-wheeled vehicles, but there are other hypotheses, including one that attributes them to the Carthaginians and their iron-rimmed wheeled carts. The ruts vary in depth (40–60cm) and width which gives credence to the idea that they were created by wooden sleds made of tree trunks, tipped with iron runners, and used to transport a variety of heavy goods and materials.

Cart ruts are found in various places in both Malta and Gozo but the largest concentration of them can be found here at Clapham Junction. The cart ruts are signposted, but when you reach the site it takes a few minutes to establish their presence. Once they are identified they take on an air of mystery. Why are they in this particular location, why do they converge, why do some disappear over the cliff edge and why are there so many of them?

### COMINO

Comino is a small – 2.5km by 2km – virtually uninhabited island sandwiched between Malta and Gozo. There are no cars or roads and only one hotel that opens for the summer. The island's history is unremarkable for it seems that only pirates were attracted to its coves and creeks and in 1618 a promontory fort, Comino Tower, was built on Comino's west side.

Unless resident at the hotel, visitors come for a day trip to enjoy the crystal-clear turquoise water or slow walks in the fresh air along vehicle-free pathways (and it is impossible to get lost!). The whole island is a wildlife sanctuary but botanically, the island is not as interesting as might be hoped, and it is not easy to find the cumin plant (*kemmuna*) from which the island receives its name. If staying on the island, there are excellent diving possibilities and even daytrippers can enjoy snorkelling if they bring their own gear.

The only significant beach area is the Blue Lagoon, formed by a channel that separates sun-baked and barren Comino from the islet of Cominotto, and only the density of bathers detracts from the intrinsic beauty of this lagoon with its fine white sand. It is essential to arrive on Comino as early as possible, especially if you want to enjoy the Blue Lagoon. Be sure to bring protective clothing, cold drinks and a picnic, although food and drinks are available at the hotel.

*Be sure to arrive early to enjoy the pleasures of Comino Island*

# West and Southwest Malta Drive

**Distance**
20km

**Time**
4–6 hours depending on visits to places of interest

**Start point**
Ċirkewwa
✚ 28A6

**End point**
Rabat & Mdina
✚ 28B3

**Lunch**
Bobbyland Bar and Restaurant
(➤ 93)

This is a chance to explore another side of Malta.

*From Valletta, drive to Ċirkewwa on the Gozo side of the isolated Marfa Peninsula. From Ċirkewwa follow the road back to Valletta until a right turn is signposted for Golden Bay and Manikata. On the road to Manikata a vista of sea suddenly appears and after 3km turn right at the unsignposted T-junction for Golden Bay.*

Detour to Golden Bay, a popular family beach. After a quick swim or lie in the sun, carry on.

*After less than 1km, at another T-junction, turn right and then straight on for Għajn Tuffieħa (➤ 49). Return to the main road and turn right, looking for a small sign on the right after 1.5km for the Roman Baths (➤ 49). After another 0.5km a detour may be made to Mġarr (➤ 61).*

Look at the 'Egg Church' and perhaps make a stop here and have lunch – the return journey is under 2km – the main road goes on to Żebbieħ and the Skorba Temples (➤ 71).

*From Żebbieħ head for Mdina (➤ 56) and then follow the signs for the Dingli Cliffs (➤ 49). Turn left at the coast, keeping the Mediterranean on your right until the road swings inland. After 1.5km take the left turn at the roundabout, signposted for Rabat, and look for an unmarked crossroads with a church on the left. A left turn at this junction leads to Verdala Palace (➤ 73).*

Stop for a tour of this cool palace if open.

*Just 1km after the Palace the first turn left leads to Buskett Gardens (➤ 46), a sign points the way on to Clapham Junction (➤ 46).*

Stretch your legs, and let yourself become absorbed in the mystery of the cart ruts. Then take the main road to Rabat.

## DINGLI CLIFFS ⭐⭐

The village of Dingli, 253m above sea level, is the highest on Malta and the nearby Dingli Cliffs offer one of the island's most stunning panoramic views. The Mediterranean appears as a vast expanse with the islet of Filfla lost out on its own. On the edge of the cliff stands the tiny and lonely chapel of St Magdalena, which dates back to 1646. Most visitors arrive in their own transport (although a bus serves Dingli village and it is a short walk to the cliffs), but the location can only really be appreciated by leaving your vehicle and taking a stroll.

➕ 28B2
✉ 15km southwest of Valletta, 4km south of Rabat
🍴 Bobbyland Bar and Restaurant (➤ 93)
🚌 81  ♿ Few
↔ Verdala Palace (➤ 73)

*The fine beach at Għajn Tuffieħa is rarely crowded*

## GĦAJN TUFFIEĦA AND GOLDEN BAY ⭐⭐

The two sandy beaches of Għajn Tuffieħa and Golden Bay, separated by a small headland, have military associations. It was in Għajn Tuffieħa that the Turkish fleet gathered before beginning the Great Siege of 1565, and the British trained their naval forces in both bays during World War II. Today, they attract mostly sun worshippers but the excavated Roman Baths near by reveal a shared concern with the serious pursuit of leisure. The baths belonged to a Roman villa, now largely disappeared but the baths were renovated by UNESCO in 1961 to show a complex that consisted of warm and cold baths, a hot-air room with underground heating and a separate small swimming pool. Occasional northwest winds create dangerous currents in the deeper parts of both bays and a red warning flag indicates the need to remain in the shallow part of the water.

➕ 28A4

**Roman Baths**

✉ Roman Baths are 1.5km from Għajn Tuffieħa on the road to Mġarr
🕐 The baths are currently closed for restoration. For more details contact Heritage Malta (☎ 22954000)
🍴 Golden Sands Hotel (£–££)
🚌 47 and 52 from Valletta, 51 from Buġibba and 652 from Sliema
♿ None  💷 Free

49

### GHARGHUR ✪✪

This small village is hidden away at the top of a ridge, and manages to evoke a sense of Malta's medieval past. If driving from Valletta, the turning off the main road is signposted for Madliena just before Splash Park (➤ 109) and the uphill trip to Għargħur is like a journey into the sealed-off past as the road winds its way over an old viaduct and up into the sun-baked countryside. The **Church of St Bartholomew** was designed by Tommaso Dingli in 1636.

Għargħur marks the northern end of the Victoria Lines and nearby Fort Madliena is part of this defensive system. From Għargħur you can either take a walk or drive inland to enjoy the spectacular scenery of the indented coastline, as well as impressive views of the Great Fault that cuts off this corner of Malta.

### GRAND HARBOUR (➤ 17, TOP TEN)

### ĦAĠAR QIM & MNAJDRA (➤ 18, TOP TEN)

### HYPOGEUM (➤ 19, TOP TEN)

### MANOEL ISLAND ✪

Connected to the mainland by a bridge, Manoel Island has an unfortunate history that seems to continue to bedevil attempts to cash in on its unquestionably prime location. The Knights of Malta used the island as a quarantine station during plagues, when it eventually could deal with up to 1,000 people at a time. The British used it as a hospital until 1940 when it then became a submarine base. Heavy bombing during World War II took its toll on Fort Manoel, which was constructed in 1732 to guard **Marsamxett Harbour**, but there are plans to renovate this highly impressive fort and create a marina.

---

✚ 29D4

**Church of St Bartholomew**
✉ 7km northwest of Valletta
🕓 Mon–Sat 4–7:30, Sun 6–11:30 and 4–7:30
🍽 Madliena Café, Caf Caf Line
🚌 55
♿ None
↔ Naxxar (➤ 62), Victoria Lines (➤ 73)

---

✚ 34B5

**Marsamxett Harbour**
✉ Between Sliema and Valletta
🍽 Cafés and restaurants (£) within walking distance on the mainland seafront
🚌 60, 61, 62 to Yacht Marina and then across the bridge
♿ None
↔ Sliema (➤ 72)

---

### Did you know?

*Malta's rigid quarantine laws made no exceptions for famous visitors. Coleridge, Thackeray and Sir Walter Scott all suffered a period of incarceration on Manoel Island which could last from 18 to 80 days, depending on where they came from. Lord Byron was especially displeased: 'Adieu, thou damned'st quarantine, that gave me fever, and the spleen.'*

## MARSASKALA ✪✪

The postcard-pretty harbour of Marsaskala (also spelt Marsascala) witnessed the last Turkish assault on Malta in 1614. Although the troops landed they were beaten back while heading inland and the Knights quickly built a mighty fort on the nearby headland to deter any future visit. Today, a tourist infrastructure is developing quickly and Marsaskala welcomes visitors with open arms. Appropriately enough, part of the fort's location has been turned into the area's premier tourist hotel, the Corinthia Jerma Palace Hotel. The village of Marsaskala has an agreeable setting by the water's edge with plenty of cafés and good seafood restaurants overlooking the bay and its pastel-coloured boats. In recent years the nightlife scene has become increasingly popular with visitors and Maltese alike. Between them, the bars and discos and an up-to-date cinema and restaurant complex appeal across the age range.

There is no beach, but nearby St Thomas Bay, 1km to the south, has sandy banks and shallow water. In summer it can seem too busy, but it is easy to escape the crowds by heading south along the coast towards Delimara Point. The road to St Thomas Bay from Marsaskala passes Mamo Tower, a 17th-century tower with an interesting cruciform design and just one room with a vaulted roof. It was privately built by a landowner to deter slave-collecting expeditions from North Africa dropping in to St Thomas Bay and abducting his peasants.

---

🞤 29F2

✉ 9km southeast of Valletta

🍴 Cafés and restaurants (£–££) by the seafront

🚌 19, 20, 22

♿ Few

↔ Marsaxlokk (➤ 55), Żabbar (➤ 78)

*The delightful resort of Marsaskala has developed across a narrow inlet on the southern coast*

# In the Know

If you only have a short time to visit Malta and Gozo, or would like to get a real flavour of the islands, here are some ideas:

## 10

### Ways to Be a Local

**Show some respect** for the virtue of patience; absolute punctuality is a worrying trait.

**Take time off** for an idle stroll along a promenade, Italian style, during the early evening hours.

**Risk a flutter** on one of the lotteries, like Super 5, and check the results on television or in the next morning's newspaper.

**Greet people** or say farewell with *sahha* (literally 'wish you good health').

**Enjoy** *pastizzi* for a morning break or late night repast.

**Browse the markets** and mingle with locals buying their fruit, vegetables, clothes and bric-à-brac.

**Observe modest dress** and behaviour in places of worship.

**Relax and chat** in a bar at any time of the day or night.

**Let time pass** over a light meal of bread, olive oil, tomatoes, vinegar and garlic in a café.

**Do not** refer to the people of Gozo as Maltese; they are Gozitans.

## 10

### Good Places To Have Lunch

**L'Ankra (££)**

✉ 11 Shore Street, Mgarr, Gozo ☎ 21555656 ⏰ Daily 11:30–2:30, 6:30–10:30. Walkable from the ferry at Mgarr harbour; good pizzas and some tasty local items like the Gozo cheese ravioli, lots of meat dishes too.

**Bloomers (££)**

✉ St George's Road, St Julian's ☎ 21333394 ⏰ Daily 12–2:30, 6:30–11:30. Easy to find on the main road, next to Melita Pharmacy, this family-run brasserie serves good Mediterranean-style food and some good salads. Daily specials.

**Café Damier (£)**

✉ Sliema Chalet Hotel, 117 Tower Road, Sliema ☎ 21335575 ⏰ 9AM–10PM. One of the more elegant places for a spot of lunch along Tower Road, with a few tables on an outdoor balcony. Pizza, pasta, burgers, salads. Good wine list.

**The Carriage (££)**

✉ Valletta Buildings, South Street, Valletta ☎ 21247828 ⏰ Mon–Fri 12–3, Fri–Sat 7:30–11. Brilliant views across to Sliema, quality food and crisp white decor combine to make The Carriage a favourite place for lunch. Superb homemade ravioli (ask, for it's not on the menu), salads and French-style dishes. Top-notch.

**Clouds Restaurant (£–££)**

✉ St George's Road, Paceville, St Julian's ☎ 99243751 ⏰ Mon–Sat 12–1AM (late at weekends). American-style restaurant in the centre of Paceville offers a relaxing lunchtime atmosphere. For a fast-food place the dishes are surprisingly tasty. Good ice-cream and milk shakes.

**Crianza (£)** ✉ 33 Archbishop Street, Valletta ☎ 21238120 ⏰ Daily 12–3:30, 6:30–11:30. Pasta, pizza (take-away available), pancakes and salads in an ancient building. Often full but worth squeezing around a table.

**It-Tmun (££)** ✉ 3 Mount Carmel Street, Xlendi, Gozo ☎ 21551571 ⏰ Wed–Mon 12–3, 6–10:30. Close to the Xlendi seafront in Gozo, this relaxing restaurant is ideal for a slow lunch. The homemade soups are very good. Outside tables offer shade.

**Pegasus (££–£££)** ✉ Le Meridien Phoenicia, The Mall, Floriana ☎ 21225241 ⏰ Mon–Sat 12–3, 6:30–10:30. The best value at this air-conditioned, brasserie-style restaurant is the set lunch. A good lunch spot; pleasantly informal.

**Porto del Sol (££)** ✉ Xemxija Road, St Paul's Bay ☎ 21573970 ⏰ Mon–Sat 12–2:30, 6–11, Sun 12–2:30. Splendid views across Xemxija Bay and carefully cooked fish, pasta and meat dishes in a comfortable and formal restaurant. Good food and wine.

**Theatru Manoel Courtyard (£)** ✉ Old Theatre Street, Valletta ☎ 21222618 🌐 Mon–Sat 11–3. A delightful little café occupying the courtyard of the theatre. Homemade pies and sandwiches; Maltese specialities; licensed.

## 10
## Top Activities

**A day by the water** in Xlendi (► 89): paddling, eating, drinking.
**Fishing off a boat** in Marsaxlokk or St Paul's Bay.
**Hiring a bicycle** in Marsalforn or Victoria to explore the country roads of Gozo (► 114).
**Hiring a car** for a day to explore the southwest corner of Malta.
**Jumping off the rocks** into the deep blue sea.
**Learning to water ski** or dive in St Julian's (► 114).
**Swimming** in the Blue Lagoon on Comino Island early in the morning.
**Taking a cruise** around the Grand Harbour and admiring the sheer size of it (► 17).
**Walking in Gozo**, especially in the Ta'Cenc area (► 87).
**Walking** the Victoria Lines (► 73).

## 10
## Best Beaches

**Armier Beach**. Situated in the extreme northeast of Malta (bus 50 from Valletta), with few facilities and occasional rough swells but lots of sand.
**Comino's beaches**. The Blue Lagoon (► 12) is deservedly the most popular spot.

**Għajn Tuffieħa Bay**. Less crowded than Golden Bay beach yet only a short walk away and reached by steps (► 49).
**Golden Bay**. The most popular beach on the island after Mellieħa Bay because of its extensive stretch of sand (► 49).
**Għejna Bay**. Without your own transport there is a 2-km walk from Malta's Mgarr, but the worthwhile reward is sand with rocky platforms.
**Marsaskala and St Thomas Bay**. There is no sand but coastal bathing is very popular here because of the bay's picturesque location.
**Mellieħa Bay**. Malta's most popular beach is 2km north of Mellieħa. Shallow water and lots of sand make it entirely suitable for children.
**Peter's Pool**. Not much of a beach but a terrific jumping-off point into crystal-clear, deep water.
**Ramla Bay**. The only really sandy beach in Gozo, shallow and safe for swimming.
**Sliema/St Julian's**. No sand but there are plenty of rocky platforms for sunbathing.

## 10
## Best Drinks and Snacks

### Drink
**Averna**. Recommended to settle the stomach after an indulgent heavy meal.

**Bajtra**. The word is Maltese for prickly pear, where this very sweet liqueur comes from. Drink when chilled.
**Fernet Branca**. Like averna, this is a 'digestive drink' taken after eating a big meal. Swallow whole, tastes foul.
**Kinnie**. Malta's very own herbal soft drink.
**Tamakari**. One of the island's most popular liqueurs. Try a tamakari kinnie cocktail – just the liqueur diluted with kinnie – ideally before an evening meal.

### Food
**Bigilla**. Bread with crushed garlic and broad beans. Sold in packets from street carts.
**Figolli**. Iced biscuits with almond and lemon, usually only available at Easter time.
**Gozo cheese**. Known as *gbejna*. The peppered version is the best, though some eat the unpeppered cheese for breakfast.
**Maltese bread**. Absolutely delicious if eaten freshly baked. If you are up early enough purchase it from the mobile breadman.
**Pastizzi**. Small savoury puff pastries filled with either local cheeses or peas.

## MARSAXLOKK ✪✪

Marsaxlokk is the largest fishing village on Malta, and the traditional and strong sense of community suggests it will remain so. Both the Turks, in 1565, and Napoleon, in 1798, landed their troops here and these days there is an annual summer invasion of tourists but Marsaxlokk retains its character and appeal. Each Sunday morning the quayside becomes an open-air fish market, and throughout the week the village's good seafood restaurants (► 94) serve the local catch.

There is no beach here, but interesting walks include a stroll to Delimara Point which passes a few bathing inlets on its eastern side. Heading south, a pleasant walk hugs the coastline as far as Birżebbuġa and takes in Għar Dalam en route.

🔲 29E2
⊠ 10km southeast of Valletta
🍴 Cafés and restaurants (£–££) by the seafront
🚌 27 from Valletta, 427 from Valletta and Buġibba, 627 from Buġibba
♿ Few
↔ Birżebbuġa (► 45), Marsaskala (► 51)

> ### *Did you know ?*
>
> *Every brightly coloured* luzzu *or fishing boat has the ever-watchful Egyptian Eye of Osiris painted on its high prow to ward off evil spirits. There may be a Catholic shrine on board as well, neatly symbolising the intertwining of cultures on Malta.*

## MELLIEĦA ✪✪

Mellieħa's popular sandy beach – the largest in Malta – is 2km north of town. It attracted Turkish pirates which led to the village of Mellieħa, which is set on a spur, being deserted in the mid-16th century. The town's present shape goes back to the 19th century when the steep main street, where houses cling to the rock, was laid out. Selmun Palace, a prominent castle with adjoining chapel, that dominates the area from its position up on the ridge, was built in the mid-18th century by Domenica Cathias. It was once owned by a charitable foundation which aimed to ransom Christian slaves who had been taken to the Barbary Coast. It is now a hotel. The heritage prize, however, goes to an ancient Marian Grotto below, near the parish church Our Lady of Victories, which has been a place of worship for centuries. The fresco of the Virgin Mary above the altar is said to have been painted by St Luke. The spring water in the Grotto is credited with medicinal powers. Mellieħa has always been a favourite with the Maltese, and is becoming popular with visitors.

🔲 28B5
⊠ 23km west of Valletta
🍴 A good choice (£–££) of cafés and restaurants
🚌 43, 44, 45 (+50 in summer) from Valletta, 48 from Buġibba and Ċirkewwa, 645 from Sliema and Ċirkewwa
♿ Few

# Mdina and Rabat

High ground away from the coast made Mdina a natural site for a defensively minded community, and Bronze Age people were probably the first to settle here. The Phoenicians and Romans knew it respectively as Maleth and Melita, and the Arabs built walls 19m high around the town they called Mdina, leaving the poorer people outside in an area that came to be known as Rabat. In the following centuries Mdina emerged as the island's capital and remained so until the Knights made Valletta the new capital in 1571.

Today, fortified medieval Mdina and Rabat should not be missed by any first-time visitor. Mdina's honey-coloured walls and narrow winding alleyways and Rabat's catacombs and Roman remains make any visit memorable.

## What to See in Mdina and Rabat

### MAGAZINE STREET AND GREEK'S GATE ✪✪

Magazine Street, so called because munitions were once stored here, borders the western side of Mdina and, unless a tour group has arrived, there is a surprising air of tranquillity to the place. There are many fine details to appreciate in the old dwellings, and photographers, if the light allows, enjoy trying to capture in close-up the brass

---

**✚** 58A2
**🍴** Cafés and restaurants (£–££) in Mdina and Rabat
**🚌** 80, 81, 84 from Valletta, 65 from Sliema and Valletta
**♿** Steps and narrow, uneven surfaces

---

**RABAT**

0    100    200 m

← Mosta

MDINA

Cathedral

Museum of Roman Antiquities

GREEK'S GATE

Palazzo Vilhena

Mgarr

TRIQ GHERIEXEM

WESGHA TAL MUZEW

MDINA GATE

Ta' Qali Crafts Village, Mosta & Valletta

TRIQ IL MUSEUM

TRIQ SANT PAWL

Loggia

Siggiewi

TRIQ L-IVITORJA

TRIQ BIR IR-RIEBU

TRIQ IL-KBIRA

TRIQ NIKOL SAURA

St Augustine's Church

RABAT

PJAZZA TAL-PAROCCA

St Paul's Church & Grotto

TRIQ SANT'AGATA

TRIQ IL-KULLEGG

St Agatha's Catacombs

St Paul's Catacombs

Buskett Gardens, Verdala Palace & Clapham Junction

A        B        C

*Entering medieval Mdina through the Greek's Gate*

knockers, the cut stone or the window mouldings. Greek's Gate is named after a small number of Greeks who came to Malta with the Knights from Rhodes and settled in this corner of Mdina. The walls of Greek's Gate are very old, dating back to Arab times. Just north of Greek's Gate is another breach in the wall, made in the 19th century for those travelling to Mdina by train. The old train station, now a restaurant, can be seen in the valley below.

## MALTA AVIATION MUSEUM ✪

Suitably located at Malta's historic World War II airport. The Spitfire and Dakota are two of the prized exhibits. You will also find a good crafts village with stalls in the original RAF nissen huts.

✛ 28C3
✉ Hut 13, Crafts Village, Ta Qali
☎ 21416095
🕐 Daily 9–5
💷 Inexpensive

## MDINA EXPERIENCE (➤ 111)

## MUSEUM OF ROMAN ANTIQUITIES ✪✪

Remains of a Roman town house were discovered just outside Mdina in 1881 and the museum is built over the site. For anyone interested in ancient Rome there are some interesting exhibits. Downstairs these include some of the original mosaics that once adorned a floor in the house, surrounded by remains of columns and busts unearthed in different corners of Malta. Noteworthy exhibits in the main gallery include an olive crusher, discovered at Marsaxlokk, used to extract the pips so oil could be made from the pulp. There is also a 2nd-century tombstone recording the death of a comedian and musician and various smaller finds.

✛ 56B2
✉ Wesgha Tal-Muzew, Rabat
☎ 21454125
🕐 16 Jun–30 Sep, Mon–Sun 7:45–2; 1 Oct–15 Jun, Mon–Sat 8:15–5, Sun 8:15–4:15
♿ No wheelchair access to the basement
💷 Inexpensive

## PALAZZO FALZON ✪✪

When Malta was under Spanish rule, the Maltese nobility emulated the architecture of the Sicilian nobility (also under Spanish rule) when building their fine homes. This style, known as Siculo-Norman, is best represented by the Palazzo Falzon, in the design of the windows and the moulding – most notably over the two doorways. The ground floor is a small private museum with naval and harbour paintings. There are displays of antique furniture and 16th- and 17th-century kitchen utensils are displayed in the charming inner courtyard.

✛ 58B3
✉ Triq Villegaignon, Mdina
☎ 21454512
🕐 Mon–Fri 10:30–1, 2:30–4:40
💷 No entrance fee but a donation is welcomed

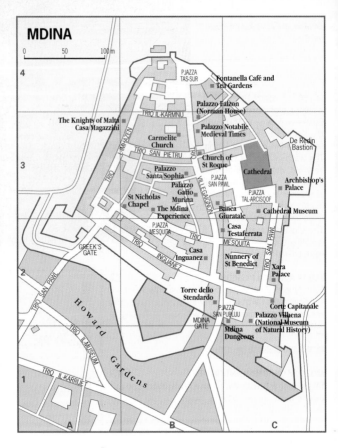

58B3

Triq Villegaignon, Mdina

## PALAZZO SANTA SOPHIA ✪

The date plaque of 1233 makes this the oldest building in Mdina. The ground floor is authentically medieval but the first floor, still true to the Siculo-Norman style, was added in 1938. Look up to the first floor level and you can see the typical horizontal moulded design known as a 'string course'. Across the road is the tiny church of St Roque, dedicated to the patron saint of diseases, which originally stood close to Mdina Gate. Grand Master de Vilhena probably did not like the idea of a church that attracted the sick set so close to his residence, Palazzo Vilhena, so he had the first church taken apart and a new one built here.

Further up the road on the other side is the Carmelite Church, not architecturally significant, but possessing some historical worth in the story of the 1798 revolt against the French, which took place after the French confiscated valuable property from the church.

## PALAZZO VILHENA/NATIONAL MUSEUM OF NATURAL HISTORY ✪

The magnificent Palazzo Vilhena, also known as the Magisterial Palace, was built by the Grand Master de Vilhena in the early 18th century. With a central courtyard, it was originally intended as his private residence. It later became an administrative building and the rear was turned into law courts, which in turn led to the basements being converted into a prison. The underground space has now been converted again to house the Mdina Dungeons (► 109). At the beginning of the 20th century the British turned the main building into a sanatorium, which it remained until the 1950s. It now houses the National Museum of Natural History.

## TALES OF THE SILENT CITY, MEDIEVAL TIMES AND THE KNIGHTS OF MALTA ✪

These multimedia shows and exhibitions, in palazzos along Villegaignon and Magazine Streets, bring to life the history and lore of Mdina, from its origins to the present day. The Knights of Malta exhibition houses around 120 life-sized figures. Available in many different languages. Entry costs are moderate.

## ST PAUL'S AND ST AGATHA'S CATACOMBS (► 24, TOP TEN)

## ST PAUL'S CATHEDRAL (► 25, TOP TEN)

## ST PAUL'S CHURCH AND ST PAUL'S GROTTO ✪✪

The original church on this site was built in 1572 but most of what you now see belongs to the late 17th century,

when it was remodelled by Lorenzo Gafa after an earthquake destroyed its predecessor. The features worth noting include the altarpiece, designed by Mattia Preti and the paintings, among which is *The Shipwreck of St Paul* by Stefano Erardi. Underneath the church is a grotto that would be unremarkable save for the legend that St Paul found shelter in this place after his shipwreck.

---

🔢 58C2
✉ St Publius Square, on the right immediately after passing through Mdina Gate
☎ 21455951 (Museum of Natural History)
🕐 16 Jun–30 Sep, Mon–Sun 7:45–2; 1 Oct–15 Jun, Mon–Sat 8:15–5, Sun 8:15–4:15
✋ Inexpensive

**Tales of the Silent City**
✉ Palazzo Gatto Murina
🔢 58B3 ☎ 21451179
🕐 Daily 9:30–4:30

**Medieval Times**
✉ Palazzo Notabile
🔢 58B3 ☎ 21454625
🕐 Mon–Sat 9:30–9:30

**Knights of Malta**
✉ Casa Magazzini
🔢 58B3 ☎ 21451342
🕐 Mon–Sat 10:30–4

🔢 56B1
✉ Pjazza Tal-Parocca, Rabat
☎ 21454467
🕐 Daily 9:15–1:30, 2–5
✋ Free

*St Paul's Church was the first on the island to be built to the design of a Latin Cross*

# A Mdina Walk

**Distance**
1km

**Time**
2–4 hours, depending on visits

**Start point**
Mdina Gate
🖪 58B2
🚌 80, 81, 83, 84, 86 from
Valletta, 65 from Sliema

**End point**
Mdina Gate
🖪 58B2

**Lunch**
Fontanella Café (£)
✉ 1 Bastion Street
☎ 454264

*The ancient streets of
Mdina were not built
for cars*

The walk begins at the Mdina Gate and immediately after passing through the gate the Mdina Dungeons (► 109), a gruesome museum, is on the right. Next door is the Palazzo Vilhena and the National Museum of Natural History (► 59).

*Take the first left and stay on this street, Triq Villegaignon, immediately passing Inguanez Street. A little way beyond, Caffè Medina brings you into Pjazza San Pawl, St Paul's Square, with a large church bearing two clocks (one of which tells the correct time; the other is there to confuse the devil). Continue along Triq Villegaignon, past a leathercraft shop, and turn left into the narrow St Peter's Street. At the bottom, turn right into Magazine Street.*

Walking along Magazine Street, you will pass the Knights of Malta exhibition (► 59) with its neat little café. There are views from the terrace here and more alfresco places up ahead which are worth a stop.

*After passing a second tea garden, walk into Bastion Square where there are views from the ramparts and places to enjoy a rest and a drink. Take the first right turning into the Triq Villegaignon.*

At the top end of the Triq Villegaignon, you first pass Palazzo Falzon (► 57) and then Medieval Times (► 59).

*Take the first left after Palazzo Notabile into the narrow St Roque Street and at the T–junction, at the bottom of the street, go left into Bastion Street and pass the entrance to Fontanella Café. Go left, take the first left into Our Savior Street and follow this street until, turning left at the T–junction, you are back on Triq Villegaignon, Mdina's main street, which leads back to the starting point.*

## What Else to See Around Malta

### MĠARR ⭐

There are not many settlements in the southwest of Malta so the farming village of Mġarr (there is a harbour with the same name in Gozo) makes a useful stop for refreshments in the course of exploring this corner of the island. It is also very close to the prehistoric sites of Skorba and Ta'Ħagrat. The town's Church of the Assumption, called the 'Egg Church', has an interesting story. In the 1930s the local priest asked the villagers to donate eggs, that could be sold for a building fund. The villagers also donated their labour, which explains why with no outside help the building work lasted from 1912 to 1946.

➕ 28B4
✉ 16km northwest of Valletta
🕐 Church daily 6–11, 4–7
🍴 A good restaurant (£–££) next to the church
🚌 47, 52
♿ Few

*Mosta's church has one of the world's largest unsupported domes*

61

### MOSTA ⭐⭐

It is the immense parish church, the Mosta Rotunda, that attracts visitors to this busy town in the centre of Malta. The Rotunda, built in the mid-19th century, has massive walls up to 6m deep and these allowed the enormous dome – the fourth largest in Europe – to be constructed without scaffolding. This amazing building feat, which lasted 27 years, was helped by the older church on the same site which was only dismantled when the new church was complete. Some question the aesthetic harmony of the two belfries and the Ionic columns of the façade fronting such a large dome, but this cannot detract from the beautiful interior with six side chapels, intricate marble floor and almost three-dimensional murals by Giuseppe Cali. The sacristy contains a replica of a 200kg bomb that pierced the dome in 1942 but fortunately failed to explode amidst the congregation. Two other bombs bounced off the dome without exploding.

### MSIDA ⭐

This once small fishing village set in a creek of Marsamxett Harbour developed into a thriving town, helped in 1989 by the building of a yacht marina, now part of Malta's main yachting marina. The parish church of St Joseph is worth a visit for its two altarpieces by Guiseppe Cali. The Ta'Xbiex Seafront, where yachts berth, offers pleasant views of Floriana across the water. There is a multitude of cafés to choose from to sit and watch the world go by.

### NAXXAR ⭐

The parish of Naxxar, on a commanding site, dates back to 1436 so, while there may be some credence to the story that after his shipwreck St Paul came here and washed his clothes out (Naxxar translates as 'to hang clothes to dry') one might wonder why he trekked 8km from the coast to do so. The quiet suburb of San Pawl tat-Tarġa ('St Paul of the Step'), where St Paul is said to have preached from the steps of the church, is only 1km away.

Palazzo Parisio, in the central square, is open to the public. Built for Grand Master Vilhena, the palazzo serves to introduce the lifestyle and surroundings of the rich nobility in 19th-century Malta.

*The graceful baroque edifice of St Joseph's Church dominates Msida Creek; the building was completed in 1892*

---

**28C3**
✉ 8km west of Valletta
☎ 21433826
🕐 Daily, 9–5 (closed during services)
🍴 Cafés and restaurants (£) near the church
🚌 43–45, 47, 49, 50 (summer only), 52 (mornings only), 56, 57, 58, 59, 65, 86, 145, 157, 159, 427
♿ Few
💲 Free
↔ Naxxar (► below)

---

**29D3**
✉ 3km southwest of Valletta
🍴 Cafés and restaurants (£) within walking distance
🚌 40–45, 47, 49, 50, 52–58, 60–64, 66–68, 141, 142, 163, 169, 452, 662, 667, 671, 672 ♿ Few
↔ Valletta (► 30–41), Sliema (► 72)

---

**28C4**
✉ 9km west of Valletta
🍴 Bars and cafés (£) across the road from the church
🚌 54, 55, 56, 59, 65, 145, 159
♿ Good
↔ Mosta (► above)

**Palazzo Parisio**
**www.**palazzoparisio.com
✉ Victory Square, Naxxar
☎ 21412461;
🕐 Mon–Fri 9–4
💲 Moderate

## QAWRA AND BUĠIBBA ✪

If you are staying in either of these tourist areas – the new promenade makes for a pleasant stroll between them – there are plenty of leisurely diversions including countless restaurants, shops, a number of bars and nightclubs, and a casino (➤ 110).

Buġibba is intensely British and UK holidaymakers will not feel homesick here. The heart of the town is in the lively Pjazza Tal-Bajja. There is no sandy beach at Buġibba but flat rocks invite sunbathing and sunbeds can be hired facing out to sea. Cruises depart from the quay next to Bognor Beach for Comino (➤ 46) and the Blue Lagoon (➤ 12). St Paul's Bay is a short walk away to the west along the coastal road.

🚩 28C5
🍴 Plenty of cafés and restaurants (£–££)
🚌 49, 70 from Valletta, 48 from Valletta and Ċirkewwa, 51 from Valletta and Għajn Tuffieħa, 652 from Sliema, 86 between Buġibba and Rabat, 427 between Buġibba and Marsaxlokk, 627 from Marsaxlokk
♿ Good
↔ St Paul's Bay (➤ 67)

✚ 29D3
✉ 4km southwest of Valletta
🍴 Nowhere suitable for a meal in the old part of town
🚌 88, 91
♿ The narrow streets are not wheelchair-friendly
↔ Valletta (➤ 30–41)

## QORMI ✪

Too many visitors travel past Qormi on their way to somewhere else, but they miss the town's medieval heritage which is reflected in the maze of very narrow streets and alleys in the old part of town, a little to the north of the modern town centre. Qormi was once known as Casal Fornaro, meaning 'Village of Bakers'. There are no special sights, although the tall church of St George is a pleasing edifice with a well-proportioned exterior that balances its façade, spires and dome. This acts as a useful landmark while exploring the nearby winding streets where one is occasionally surprised by a lovely 16th-century house with an ornate balcony.

✚ 29D1
✉ 11km southwest of Valletta
🍴 Only a couple of bars (£)
🚌 35, 138
♿ Good
↔ Ħagar Qim & Mnajdra (➤ 18), Blue Grotto (➤ 45), Żurrieq (➤ 79)

## QRENDI ✪✪

This is the perfect village for those who like to seek out relatively unimportant places of antique interest. The diminutive Church of St Catherine Tat-Torba is worth a visit if only to wonder at its unique façade. Another oddity, for Malta, is the octagonal Gwarena Tower, while to the south of the village there is a natural wonder known as Il-Maqluba. This huge hole in the soft limestone, some 100m across and 50m deep, was caused presumably by the collapse of a subterranean cave. This gave rise to an unflattering legend concerning the people of Qrendi: the inhabitants were so ungodly that they and their village were cast into hell, via Il-Maqluba, but even the devil rejected them and the tangled mass was cast into the sea thus creating the islet of Filfla.

*The village of Qrendi prepares for a festival procession*

# North Coast Drive

The North Coast was where St Paul was shipwrecked and where both the Turks and Napoleon landed.

*Follow Tower Road in Sliema in the direction of St Julian's, following the signs for St Paul's Bay and Mellieħa.*

Once outside the town the first stopping point is the unsignposted village of Għargħur (➤ 50).

*To reach it, turn left at the turning for Madliena which is signposted (if you pass Splash Park you have gone too far) and follow the winding road up to Għargħur.*

Soak up the atmosphere of this ancient elevated village with fine views.

*Retrace your route to the main road and turn left to continue travelling west towards St Paul's Bay.*

The road hugs the coast as far as Salina Bay before reaching Buġibba and St Paul's Bay (➤ 67). A walk along the promenade in St Paul's should give one an appetite for lunch.

*After lunch drive the short distance further west to Mellieħa (➤ 55), stopping perhaps at the island's largest sandy beach, which is just 2km north of the town, descending the ridge. From the beach continue on to the northwest corner of Malta, the Marfa Ridge, and photogenic Ċirkewwa, from where the ferries depart for Gozo.*

There are a number of small beaches near here which, outside weekends, attract few visitors.

*From Ċirkewwa head back to Mellieħa and turn right at the main roundabout to head south to Għajn Tuffieħa (➤ 49). From here take the main road to Żebbieħ, Mosta and Naxxar (➤ 62). From Naxxar it is a short distance back to Sliema.*

**Distance**
40km

**Time**
6–8 hours

**Start point**
Sliema
🚹 29E4

**End point**
Sliema
🚹 29E4

**Lunch**
Gillieru Restaurant, St Paul's Bay (££–£££)
☎ 21573480

## ST JULIAN'S, PACEVILLE AND ST GEORGE'S BAY ✪✪

St Julian's was a sleepy fishing village that awoke one day in 1798 to find nearly 500 of Napoleon's ships in the bay. The French invasion was largely unopposed and 200 years later a different kind of invasion takes place each summer when thousands of visitors of all nationalities visit. Their arrival is welcomed because St Julian's, sometimes seen as just an extension of Sliema, is a major tourist centre in its own right. It is attractively located along the line of the two curving bays of Balluta and St Julian's (sometimes called Spinola) and its promenade is a continuation of Tower Road in Sliema.

Beyond St Julian's is a small promontory where Paceville is located. Paceville (pronounced patch-e-ville) is the nightlife capital of Malta and when darkness falls neon lights illuminate the discos, pubs and cafés that jostle for space and customers. The latest addition to the entertainment scene is Bay Street, a modern complex of trendy shops, cafés and restaurants, with a bowling alley and a multi-screen cinema complex near by (▶ 108).

Around the headland of Dragonara Point is St George's Bay, the only local beach area and consequently very popular. The sandy part of the beach is minute and, although the number of bobbing boats makes any kind of water activity difficult, the setting is very attractive and there are lidos near by. The far side of St George's Bay is developing into a mass of top-notch hotels, which are dominated by the San Gorg hotel, and there are a number of quality restaurants.

### ST PAUL'S BAY ✪✪

This premier resort area stretches from Mistra Bay on the west side of St Paul's Bay down to the mouth of the bay via Xemxija and up through Buġibba to Qawra on the east side of St Paul's. The sun, good beaches, beautiful water and seaside fun atmosphere combine to make it a mass-market destination. The original village of St Paul's Bay covers the area between Għajn Razul and St Paul's Church, for the saint was shipwrecked here in AD 60. The elegant church of St Paul was built where he lit a bonfire and threw a viper into it, thus miraculously expelling all the poison from Malta's snakes. About 1.5km from the church, on the left side of the main road in the direction of Xemxija, is Għajn Razul (the Apostle's Fountain). Here St Paul baptised the first Maltese or, according to another legend, it is the site where he struck a rock and water poured forth. A Grand Master created the shrine and his coat of arms adorns the façade.

🚏 29D4
✉ 7km northwest of Valletta
🍽 Plenty of cafés and restaurants (£–£££) in the area
🚌 62, 64–66, 68, 70, 667, 671 from Valletta, 627 between Paceville and Marsaxlokk
♿ Few
🚢 Sliema (▶ 72)

*St Paul's Bay (opposite) and Spinola Bay are home to two of Malta's premier resorts*

🚏 28B5
✉ 19km northwest of Valletta
🍽 Plenty of cafés and restaurants (£–££) along the seafront
🚌 43-4, 45, 48, 49, 50, 52, 145, 159 from Valletta, 48 from Valletta and Ċirkewwa, 86 from Buġibba
♿ Good
🚢 Qawra & Buġibba (▶ 63)

# Food & Drink

Hotels and restaurants serve a large range of international cuisines ranging from Italian to the oriental, with a strong British contribution along the lines of roast beef and apple pie. Less ostentatiously displayed but well worth seeking out are the local establishments which serve the traditional home cooking of the islands.

## Maltese Cuisine

Maltese food owes much to the many cultures of the peoples who have occupied or traded with the island over the centuries. Like Italian food it often uses pasta, and like Moorish food it relies on spicy sauces, but it has a quality of its own which has evolved from the special circumstances of the island. Many vegetables can be grown all year round while fish tends to be seasonal. The shortage of firewood for ovens in the past meant that food was cooked slowly in earthenware pots or taken to the village baker to be roasted. Despite the advent of modern stoves these styles of cooking are still preferred and they too influence the taste of the food.

*The simple pleasure of delicious fresh bread is a daily blessing in Malta and Gozo*

Pastry is a common element. Combinations of meat or fish with vegetables and cheeses are encased in shortcrust or filo-type pastry. A traditional dish is

the Sicilian *timpana*, a mixture of meat, liver, tomatoes, eggs and pasta with a pastry crust. *Stuffat tal-laham* is a thick, traditional, beef stew made using topside or rump plus whatever vegetables and seasonings are at hand.

Traditional soups are often based on fish with garlic, tomatoes and marjoram. A traditional spring vegetable soup is *kusksu*, made with broad beans, pasta and tomatoes. Look out too for *aljotta*, a fish soup that takes its name from the Italian *aglio* (garlic) which always makes its presence felt in this dish. There is also *soppa ta l-armla*, widow's soup, which uses a mixture of vegetables, tomato paste and eggs, served with cheese and thick slices of local bread.

Traditional meat dishes which should be tried include stewed rabbit cooked in wine and *bragjoli*, little parcels of stuffing wrapped in slices of beef and slowly simmered.

## Vegetable Dishes

The range of vegetables is extraordinary and because of the traditional abstinence from meat on Fridays many vegetable dishes are available. The Maltese version of ratatouille is called *kapunata*, a mix of garlic, aubergine and peppers. Savoury pumpkin pie is popular as are spinach and anchovy pies. There is even a Maltese version of minestrone called *minestra* – made with at least eight vegetables – which is often more like a thick vegetable stew than its Italian counterpart. Accompanied by the excellent Maltese bread, soups make a satisfying meal.

Desserts and sweets are popular, sometimes spectacular, but rarely like the pastries of other European cuisines. On the street, especially during a festival, home-made nougat, iced biscuits stuffed with almond paste (*figoli*) or fresh fruit are sold. Also eaten during festivals is *prinjolata*, a dessert made from a pyramid of sponge fingers, almond cream, chocolate and cherries. Bakeries sell delicious filled pastries while restaurants offer *helwa tat-Tork,* which is a crushed mix of sugar and almonds.

## Alcoholic Drinks

Local wine is cheap and mostly quite cheerful, but beware of the high alcohol content. Local beers are Hopleaf, and Blue Label and Cisk lager. Lowenbrau and Stella Artois are available. Small cafés usually sell alcohol, and bars sell food and beverages.

*Marsovin and Delicata are the two main producers of wine in Malta and Marsovin's Marnisi wine is worth trying. There is also the smaller Meridiana company (www.meridiana.com.mt) producing wine from 100 per cent Maltese grapes and their Isis (chardonnay) is one of the best Maltese wines.*

## SENGLEA

Senglea, on a peninsula separating two waterways, is one of the historic Three Cities, along with Vittoriosa and Cospicua, where the Knights first settled after 1530. It was almost completely destroyed in World War II. The Safe Haven Gardens at the promontory's tip, the northern end of Victory Street, are worth a visit. From the lookout in the gardens there is a truly spectacular view of the Grand Harbour with Vittoriosa's Fort Angelo over to the right and Valletta's mighty walls straight across the water. The stone vedette at the tip carries a sculptured eye and ear, symbols of vigilance.

## SIĠĠIEWI

This village, one of 10 original parishes, had a population of 1,500 when the Knights arrived in 1530. It has one of the foremost baroque churches on the island. The dominating Church of St Nicholas was built in the last quarter of the 17th century with two aisles and a dome added in the 19th century. The richly embellished interior includes an altar-piece that is the last, unfinished, work by Preti.

Under 5km to the west of Siġġiewi the attractively located Inquisitor's Summer Palace, built in 1625 by Inquisitor Visconti, may be viewed, but not visited as it is now a summer home for the prime minister. Some 4km to the south of Siġġiewi, on the coast, is Għar Lapsi. There is no sand but it is a popular swimming spot with Maltese families and there is a footpath to the Blue Grotto (➤ 45).

*Siġġiewi's Church of St Nicholas looks out at a huge stone statue of the titular saint*

---

+ 29E3

☒ 4km (by road) south of Valletta

🍴 Café (£) near the church but consider a picnic

🚌 3

♿ Good

---

+ 28C2

☒ 8km southwest of Valletta

🍴 A bar (£) in Siġġiewi serves snacks and there is a restaurant (£) at Għar Lapsi

🚌 89, 94

♿ Few

↔ Ħagar Qim (➤ 18), Buskett Gardens (➤ 46)

### SKORBA AND TA'HAGRAT ✪

These two archaeological sites may appear to be just a collection of old stones, but both have revealed important clues to Malta's prehistory. The Skorba site was excavated in the 1960s and the finds of pottery, animal bones and wheat make it likely that this was a Neolithic and Bronze Age dwelling place.

The Ta'Hagrat site, in the centre of Mgarr, revealed evidence of temples that are contemporary with Ggantija. This makes it the earliest standing temple site in Malta, and both sites, with Ggantija, are the oldest standing monuments in the world.

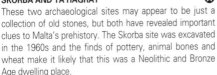

> ### Did you know ?
>
> *St Luke, who accompanied St Paul,
> recorded their arrival:
> 'And the barbarous people [living near what is
> now St Paul's Bay] shewed us no little kindness:
> for they kindled a fire, and received us every
> one, because of the present rain and because of
> the cold.'* Acts of the Apostles: 28: 1–2

☩ 28B4

✉ Skorba is signposted on the left before Żebbiefi on the road from Mgarr. Ta'Hagrat is a short walk from the centre of Mgarr

🍴 A good restaurant (£) in Mgarr near the church

🚌 47

♿ Ta'Hagrat may be viewed from the outside but Skorba is more difficult to approach

↔ Ghajn Tuffieħa and Golden Bay (► 49)

❓ Ta'Hagrat is open by appointment only. Contact Heritage Malta (☎ 21239545)

Senglea viewed across the Grand Harbour from a Valletta lookout

**+** 29E4

**✉** 7km from Valletta

**🍴** Plenty of cafés and restaurants (£–££)

**🚌** 61, 62, 64, 65, 67, 68, 70, 671 from Valletta for ferries, also 60, 63, 163 from Valletta, 70 from Buġibba, 65 from Rabat, 86 from Buġibba and Rabat, 645 from Ċirkewwa, 652 from Golden Bay

**⛴** Valletta–Sliema ferry (☎ 23463333)

**♿** Generally manageable along Tower Road and The Strand but the side streets are often steep and difficult to manage

**↔** St Julian's, Paceville and St George's Bay (➤ 67)

*Space on land, at least, is at a premium in up-market Sliema*

## SLIEMA ✪✪

Sliema is an affluent and fashionable residential area for the Maltese and a prime holiday base for tourists thanks to a number of top- and middle-range hotels. Tower Road is its 5-km promenade, full of shops and restaurants, and the road continues north to St Julian's and Paċeville. Sliema has no sandy beaches but swimming and bathing off the rocky platforms along Tower Road is popular and there is a lido farther along the road. The southern end of Tower Road joins The Strand, which fronts Sliema Creek. A short way along The Strand, at a transport point known as The Ferries, there is a bus terminus, a regular 5-minute ferry service to Valletta, Captain Morgan cruises to Comino and elsewhere (➤ 110), a catamaran service to Gozo and, further down the road, the bridge to Manoel Island (➤ 50). At night there are atmospheric views of Valletta across the water from The Strand, always a popular place for Maltese residents to stroll and chat. The side streets into residential Sliema do not lead to any specific sights, but a meandering walk should throw up some of the fine villas built by the Maltese bourgeoisie at the beginning of the 20th century.

The Tigne headland offered the best point for guarding Marsamxett Harbour and Valletta, although the Knights did not build a fort here until 1792. Other forts are dotted along the coastline and one of them is now a popular restaurant on Tower Road.

## TARXIEN TEMPLES (▶ 26, TOP TEN)

### VERDALA PALACE ✪

This castle-like palace was built in 1586 by a Grand Master as a summer residence and now, as a seasonal home for the president, performs a similar kind of function. It has been renovated and enriched over the centuries but the luxury of its interior cannot be seen by visitors unless it once again opens to the public on certain days of the week.

### VICTORIA LINES ✪✪

There is a natural fault line running across Malta, the Great Fault, and the Knights were the first to capitalise on the defensive capabilities of this rift in the land that reaches 239m. They built watchtowers in gaps in the fault and later the British reinforced these, added more, and linked them up with a stonework parapet before officially christening them the Victoria Lines. Given their commanding position, the Victoria Lines offer scenic views across to Gozo and a focus for short walks in Malta's countryside. A recommended 3-km stretch is that between Nadur (west of Rabat) and Falka Gap, and the Lines can also be reached from Għargħur, Mġarr, Mosta and Naxxar.

*Verdala Palace*

✚ 28C2
⊠ 3km southeast of Rabat
🚌 81
🔁 Buskett Gardens (▶ 46), Clapham Junction (▶ 46), Dingli Cliffs (▶ 49)

✚ 28B4/C4
⊠ From Fomm ir-Rih (southwest of Mġarr) to Fort Madliena (northeast of Għargħur)
🍴 Bring a picnic or eat in Mġarr, Mosta or Naxxar (£–££)
🚌 47 to Mġarr, 49, 53, 56 to Mosta, 55 to Għargħur and Naxxar
♿ None

73

# Vittoriosa

In 1530 the Knights of the Order of St John chose a settlement on a narrow peninsula of land overlooking the creeks of the Grand Harbour as their headquarters, and set about fortifying it. Then known as Birgu, in 1565 the town was besieged for three months by the Turks and, though many lives were lost, the town was not taken. After the siege the Knights began the construction of a new capital but Birgu was given the name Vittoriosa – the victorious one – as an accolade. Many of the early buildings and fortifications of the Knights are still here along with narrow winding streets, and there are many reminders of the second great siege during World War II.

## What to See in Vittoriosa

### CHURCH OF ST LAWRENCE ⭐⭐

Originally built in the 11th century, this historically important church was rebuilt in 1530 by the Knights of St John as their Conventual Church. In 1691 it was virtually reconstructed by Lorenzo Gafa (builder of the cathedrals at Mdina and Victoria on Gozo) in the baroque style. The well balanced and impressive exterior with twin clock towers and dome is matched by a lavish dimly lit interior. The church was damaged during World War II but the reconstruction and repairs are faithful to the original. Red marble and frescoes by Cortis and Joseph Calli adorn the walls and the ceiling. The most important work displayed in the chapel is a depiction of the martyrdom of St Lawrence by Mattia Preti.

*The hat and sword of Grand Master La Valette are exhibited in the chapel of the Church of St Lawrence*

➕ 35F1/29E3
✉ Triq San Lawrenz, Vittoriosa
☎ 21827057
🕐 Mon–Sun 6–10, 4–7
🍴 Café Riche (£) (▶ 98)
🚌 1, 2, 4, 6
♿ Good
💲 Free
❓ Festival of St Lawrence, 10 August

# A Walk in Vittoriosa

The old capital has both impressive sites and tiny, homely stores and shops on this important promontory in Grand Harbour.

*Enter Vittoriosa through the main gate, the Gate of Provence, which leads directly to the main street, Triq il-Mina-Kbira.*

On the right the Inquisitor's Palace (➤ 77) is passed and soon after the street enters Victory Square (➤ 77).

*Keep on your left for St Joseph's Oratory (➤ 77) and take the nearby turning out of the Square on Triq Nestu Laiviera and down the stepped pavement for St Lawrence's Church (➤ 74).*

With your back to the church entrance, turn right at the water's edge and pass through the gate, pausing to admire the splendid Canaletto-like view across the water.

*Passing the Maritime Museum (➤ 77) on the right, walk along the quayside past the boats and ships and cross the small bridge at the end before walking up the broad ramp to Fort St Angelo (➤ 76).*

Stop to admire the views on both sides and maybe take a photograph.

*Retrace your steps to Victory Square and, from the position where you first entered the Square along Triq il-Kbira, take the narrow turning in the right corner (which has a street sign saying Block 5).*

The *auberges* (none open) were the first, more humble, ones of the Order. Go straight down this narrow lane, passing the Auberge d'Angleterre on the right.

*At the end turn right and follow the street uphill until a fork is reached. Bear to the right and go along this street, Pacifiku Scicluna, to the end where you turn right at the T-junction. Then take the next left to enter once more the main street, Triq il-Kbira, which leads back to the gate where you entered Vittoriosa. Café Riche is on the left after leaving through the gate.*

*A fine example of vernacular architecture in Victory Square in Vittoriosa*

**Distance**
1.5km

**Time**
2–4 hours, depending on church and museum visits

**Start point**
Main gate entrance to Vittoriosa
➕ 35F1
🚌 1, 2, 4, 6

**End point**
Main gate entrance to Vittoriosa
➕ 35F1

**Lunch**
Café Riche (£)
✉ Cospicua
☎ 21820989
❓ A tourist board brochure, *A Walking Tour of the Cottonera*, includes a map of Vittoriosa

35F1

✉ Vittoriosa Wharf

🕐 Currently closed for restoration

🍴 Café Riche (£)

🚌 1, 2, 4, 6

🎫 Inexpensive. Ticket covers Fort St Elmo (► 38)

♿ Some uneven surfaces

*The defences of Fort St Angelo are clearly visible from Valletta*

### FORT ST ANGELO ✪

Records show that a fort called Castrum Maris stood on the site of Fort Angelo in 1274 but it is believed that a building was here long before that, possibly a temple to the Phoenician goddess Asthart. In 1530 it became the seat of the Grand Master and the Knights added more fortifications which withstood the Great Siege. When the siege ended the great bell was rung continuously for a day. Later the fort became a prison where rebellious Knights were held. There are two chapels inside the fortress, one a 12th-century building dedicated to the Virgin Mary and the other a 16th-century building dedicated to St Anne. The early Grand Masters are buried here, as are many of the Knights who died defending the city. The fort was the British naval headquarters and the base for Allied naval operations in the Mediterranean during World War II.

## THE INQUISITOR'S PALACE ✪✪

This building began its life in the Norman period as the Court of Justice but was enlarged and taken over when the Papal Inquisition came to Malta in 1574. The 62 Inquisitors sat here and an unknown number of people were tortured and died at their hands. Two of the Inquisitors went on to become popes, Alexander VII and Innocent XII. In the museum are exhibits of household utensils, tools, furniture and craft paraphernalia. The dungeons with prisoners' graffiti are still there, as are the courtrooms and the Inquisitors' chapel. One wing of the building dates back to the original Norman structure.

🔤 35F1
✉ Main Gate Street
☎ 21663731
🕐 Daily 9–5
🍴 Café Riche (£)
🚌 1, 2, 4, 6
♿ None
🎫 Inexpensive

## THE MARITIME MUSEUM ✪✪

The walls are decorated with pictures of the hundreds of ships which have played a part in Malta's history while the various rooms effectively display different eras in naval history. There are Roman anchors, models of the ships of the Order of St John and Royal Navy vessels as well as models of the tiny *luzzu* (► 55) which still bob about the harbour, medieval navigating equipment, cannon and ancient uniforms.

🔤 35F1
✉ Vittoriosa Wharf
☎ 21660052
🕐 Daily 9–5
🍴 Café Riche (£)
🚌 1, 2, 4, 6
♿ None 🎫 Inexpensive

## ST JOSEPH'S ORATORY ✪✪

This tiny, interesting museum is set in a little square outside the north door of the Church of St Lawrence. Exhibits include the hat and sword worn by Grand Master La Vallette, and curiosities ranging from long wafer-holding tongs used by the priests to give communion when there was a plague, an ancient crucifix used at public executions, and an early Bible used by the Inquisitors, to a much-used pack of playing cards of 1609.

🔤 35F1
✉ Vittoriosa Square
🕐 Mon–Sat 8:30–12, 2– 4, Sun 9:30–12
🍴 Café Riche (£)
🚌 1, 2, 4, 6
♿ Few
🎫 Free

## VICTORY SQUARE ✪

This square was the centre of social life here in Vittoriosa for centuries. In it is the Victory Monument, erected in 1705, a statue of St Lawrence and a stone crucifix marking the spot where executions took place. On 10 August this square comes alive at the Festival of St Lawrence. Around the square are the *auberges* of Germany, England (which never moved to Valletta because of the Reformation) and Auvergne, but these *auberges* are modest compared to the grand ones in Valletta.

🔤 35F1
✉ Vittoriosa Square
🍴 Café Riche (£)
🚌 1, 2, 4, 6
♿ Good

## VITTORIOSA 1565 MUSEUM ✪

Celebration of the 1565 siege depicting Turks scaling walls and brave Knights defending their city. Open Mon–Sat 9–2:30 (4 in winter), Sun 9–1.

🔤 35F1
✉ 24 Wenzu Dyer Street
☎ 21891565

## What Else to See Around Malta

### ŻABBAR ★

➕ 29E3
✉ 7km southeast of Valletta
☎ 21824383 (church museum)
🕐 Sun 9–12 (church museum)
🍴 Apart from a café (£) at the end of Santiwarju Street near the church, there is not much choice
🚌 18, 19, 21, 22, 23
♿ Few
💷 Free (church museum)
↔ Marsaskala (▶ 51)

The Turks set up camp here on the dawn of the Great Siege, when the then village lay just outside the later Cottonera Lines, the fortified walls protecting the Three Cities, where the Knights first settled. When the French were blockaded behind the Lines in 1800 the village of Żabbar became the focus for the Maltese military opposition. French cannon fire did serious damage to the Church of Our Lady of Graces but the restored church is worth a visit. Originally designed by Tommaso Dingli in 1640, the impressive ceiling of the nave is his only intact work. The exterior façade is a good example of over-the-top baroque. On Sunday mornings the church opens a small ecclesiastical museum with a number of votive paintings. East of town the Hompesch Arch, which is forlornly placed in the middle of a road junction, is a sad reminder of Malta's last Grand Master, who surrendered to Napoleon.

> ### Did you know ?
>
> Grand Masters ruled Malta from 1530 to 1798 but only the last one (1797–98), Ferdinand von Hompesch from Germany, bothered to learn the Maltese language. He was also the only German Grand Master. A weak leader, but a kind man, he learned the language because he respected the Maltese.

### ŻEBBUĠ ★

➕ 28C3
✉ 8km southwest of Valletta
🍴 Nowhere suitable for a meal
🚌 88
♿ Few

The town of Żebbuġ, one of the original 10 parishes of 1486, is indifferent to tourism and few visitors bother stopping other than those seeking out interesting old churches. The Church of St Philip, built in 1632 in the town square, is the most impressive place of worship, designed by the son of the famous Gerolamo Cassar, who was so influential in the building of Valletta. There are similarities with St John's Co-Cathedral.

More difficult to find is the tiny Church of Tal-Hlas, tucked away to the north of the town centre, worth seeking out for its barred iron windows in the façade. This useful feature protected the priest during pirate raids, while he said Mass for his much less fortunate parishioners outside.

# Gozo

Gozo is only 14km long by 7km wide, one third the size of Malta, but the island is no mere adjunct. The prehistoric stones of Ġgantija testify  to its long history, and the mighty citadel at Victoria demonstrates how important it was to both the Arabs and the Romans. Today, the island is grappling with the dilemma of encouraging its tourist industry while trying to preserve the traditional way of life that draws visitors here in the first place. The balance is still a healthy one.

There is only one sandy beach and no obvious resort areas, so visitors should not come expecting to find cosmopolitan distractions. The pace of life is slower in this agricultural and fishing community, which is the essence of Gozo's appeal. Fewer and smaller roads, less sense of congestion and a calmer atmosphere and superb swimming and diving combine to produce a place of escape and relaxation.

> *'Its coast scenery may truly be called pomskizillious and gromphibberous, being as no words can describe its magnificence.'*

EDWARD LEAR
Letter to Lady Waldegrave (1866)

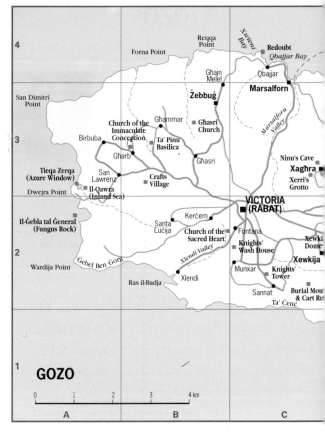

**GOZO**

0   1   2   3   4 km

|  | A | B | C |

*(map labels)*

Reqqa Point
Forna Point
Xatieni Bay
Redoubt
*Qbajjar Bay*
Ghajn Melel
Qbajjar
**Marsalforn**
**Żebbuġ**
San Dimitri Point
Ghammar
**Ghasri Church**
*Marsalforn Valley*
Church of the Immaculate Conception
Birbuba
**Ta' Pinu Basilica**
Ghasri
Ninu's Cave
**Xagħra**
Gharb
San Lawrenz
**Crafts Village**
**Xerri's Grotto**
Tieqa Żerqa (Azure Window)
Dwejra Point
Il-Qawra (Inland Sea)
**VICTORIA (RABAT)**
Il-Ġebla tal Ġeneral (Fungus Rock)
Santa Luċija
Kerċem
Church of the Sacred Heart
Fontana
Knights' Wash House
**Xewkija Dome**
*Gebel Ben Gorg*
*Xlendi Valley*
Munxar
Knights' Tower
**Xewkija**
Wardija Point
Ras il-Badja
Xlendi
Sannat
Burial Mou & Cart Ru
Ta' Ċenċ

*The domed church of St George dominates the skyline of Victoria (Rabat) in Gozo*

# Victoria (Rabat)

Gozo's capital was called simply Rabat ('the town') until 1897, when a British Governor changed the name at the time of Queen Victoria's Diamond Jubilee, but the old name also remains in use.

The hilltop Citadel (Il-Kastell) is the focus of most visitors' interest and has a cathedral and museums. Victoria itself is a pleasant little town with a church worth seeing and a central square that buzzes with life in the morning before falling asleep during the afternoon. The central square, It-Tokk ('the meeting place'), has some tiny bars where one may sit and watch the gentle routine of Gozitan life, while a mysterious maze of narrow little streets and alleyways radiates out from the square.

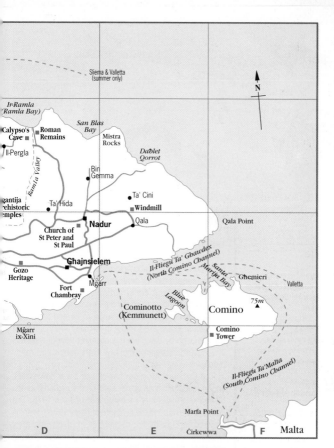

Sliema & Valletta
(summer only)

N

Ir-Ramla
(Ramla Bay)

Calypso's
Cave

Roman
Remains

Il-Pergla

San Blas
Bay

Mistra
Rocks

Daħlet
Qorrot

Bin
Gemma

Ta' Cini

**Ġgantija
Prehistoric
Temples**

Ramla Valley

Ta' Ħida

**Windmill**

**Nadur**

Church of
St Peter and
St Paul

Qala

Qala Point

**Għajnsielem**

Gozo
Heritage

Mġarr

Il-Fliegu Ta' Għawdex
(North Comino Channel)

Santa
Marija Bay

Għemieri

Valletta

Fort
Chambray

Mġarr
ix-Xini

Cominotto
(Kemmunett)

Blue
Lagoon

Comino

75m

Comino
Tower

Il-Fliegu Ta'Malta
(South Comino Channel)

Marfa Point

D

E

Ċirkewwa

F

Malta

## What to See in Victoria (Rabat)

+ 85B3

**Folklore Museum, Archaeological Museum and Natural Science Museum**
- ☎ 21556144
- ⏲ Daily 9–5
- 🍴 Cafés and restaurants (£–££) within walking distance
- ♿ Few
- 💶 Inexpensive
- ↔ Gozo Cathedral (➤ 85)

**Victoria Tourist Office**
- ✉ Tigrija Palazz, Republic Street
- ☎ 21561419
- ⏲ Mon–Fri 9–5, Sat–Sun 9–12:30

### THE CITADEL ✪✪✪

The origins of this fortified enclave go back to Gozo's early history under Roman and Arab occupation. In 1551 Turkish raiders penetrated its defences and soon after this the Knights set about constructing sturdy bastions and ordering all Gozitans to spend their nights inside its walls – a policy that did not officially come to an end for almost 100 years. Now, the Citadel is virtually uninhabited at night, though by day there is a constant flow of travellers visiting the cathedral, the few craft shops and many museums.

The Cathedral Museum has church silver downstairs, ecclesiastical paintings upstairs and on the ground floor the bishop's 19th-century carriage, last used in 1975. The **Folklore Museum** is the favourite of many visitors with its down-to-earth collection of practical artefacts, including two splendid mills. The **Archaeological Museum** has an important collection of Roman remains and Gozitan antiquities and, if time is limited, this and the Folklore Museum are the two worth seeing. An interesting exhibit is a 12th-century Arabic tombstone, inscribed in Kufic characters, mourning the premature death of a young Muslim girl. The **Natural Science Museum** has an unsurprising collection with the usual array of stuffed birds and geological exhibits. The **Armoury** is a disappointment because one can only peer through a gate at the exhibits. The **Craft Centre** has displays of local pottery, glass, wrought iron and lace, which are not for sale but may whet your shopping appetite for the goods in some of the small craft shops inside the Citadel.

Many of the buildings inside the Citadel were destroyed by Dragut, in the seige of 1551, and in an earthquake of 1693, but the whole complex has been sympathetically restored and a walk around the ramparts offers terrific views while evoking a sense of Gozo's ancient past.

*There are good views of Gozo from the Citadel's 400-year-old walls, here looking east*

## GOZO CATHEDRAL ✪✪

The entrance to the Citadel in Victoria leads into a piazza with broad steps occupying most of one side, which lead up to the cathedral dedicated to the Assumption of Our Lady. The exterior is perfectly proportioned, as befits a building designed by Lorenzo Gafa, but there is no dome where Gafa intended one. Visual compensation is provided inside: the flat roof has the illusion of a dome painted onto it, this *trompe l'oeil* being an outstanding feature.

✚ 85B2
✉ The Citadel
☎ 21556087
🕐 Museum: Mon–Sat 10–1, 1:30–4:30
🍴 Cafés and restaurants (£–££) within walking distance
♿ Good
🎟 Inexpensive
↔ The Citadel (➤ 84)

## ST GEORGE'S CHURCH ✪✪

This lavishly decorated church, also known as the Basilica of St George, was built in 1678 after a design by Vittorio Cassar but with many alterations since, including a new façade in the 19th century and the addition of a dome and aisles in the 20th century. The interior is richly adorned, with a wealth of baroque trappings. The altar has alabaster decorated columns supporting a canopy, a diminutive copy of Bernini's in St Peter's in Rome. Some interesting art work includes a wooden statue of St George by Gozitan artist Paola Azzopardi that was carved from a single tree. The altarpiece is by Mattia Preti and the vault paintings are by Conti. The third Sunday in July celebrates the saint.

✚ 85B1
✉ St George's Square
☎ 21556377
🕐 Daily, 4:30AM–1PM, 3:30–7
🍴 Cafés and restaurants (£–££) within walking distance
♿ None
🎟 Free
↔ The Citadel (➤ 84)

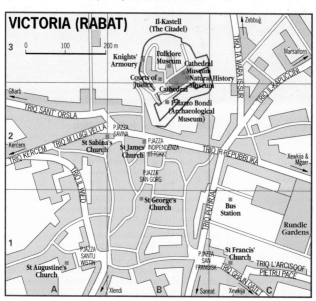

VICTORIA (RABAT)

## What Else to See Around Gozo

### THE AZURE WINDOW AND THE FUNGUS ROCK ⚫⚫

The natural phenomenon of *Il-Qawra* (Inland Sea) is a land-locked seawater pool but with a natural tunnel in the rock that allows the sea water in. A boat trip through the tunnel brings one to a door-like opening in the cliff through which one gazes at the Mediterranean. To Gozitans it has always been known as *Tieqa Zerqa* – the Azure Window – because of the colour of the dark blue sea. Near by, off Dwejra Point, there is a rocky outcrop in the sea known as Fungus Rock.

 82A3

✉ 2km west of San Lawrenz

🍴 Drinks and snacks (£) available in the car park area

🚌 91 from Victoria

♿ None

💷 Inexpensive

### ĠGANTIJA TEMPLES (➤ 16, TOP TEN)

### MARSALFORN ⚫⚫

The fishing village of Marsalforn was popular with those Gozitans who could afford a summer break long before it was discovered by tourists. It is the island's only resort area but a fairly low-key one compared with somewhere like St Julian's or St Paul's in Malta. There are waterside restaurants, bars and hotels, boat trips, and water activities can be arranged here. Bicycles can be hired in the village and, given the small size of Gozo, this opens up a lot of possibilities. A drawback to Marsalforn is that there is not much of a beach, but it is only a short walk to the nearby bays of Qbajjar and Xwejni and here visitors will have a bit more space.

🔳 82C4

✉ 4km north of Victoria

🍴 Cafés and restaurants (£–££) on the quayside

🚌 21 from Victoria

♿ Good

*More of a door than a window, the Azure Window beckons to the blue expanse beyond*

# A Walk Around Gozo

For a walk in southern Gozo, drive or take a bus to Sannat, the most southerly village, close to the Ta'Cenc cliffs.

*At the southern end of Sannat follow the signposted left turnings to Ta'Cenc/Dolmen/ Cliffs. If driving, park where the last sign points left.*

You will find a fine view of Xewkija's domed church, The Rotunda (▶ 89), dominating the plain on your left. There is also a superb view of Victoria's acropolis, the Citadel.

*You arrive at a crossroad of sorts (the roads have recently been surfaced) where you turn left, and not straight on which leads down to the sea and a small private beach belonging to the hotel.*

The road you are on has a view of Comino and the western coastline of Malta up ahead in the distance, while all around is Gozo's barren landscape of limestone and scrubland. In this vicinity there are cart ruts (▶ 46) and Neolithic burial mounds, but they are not signposted and it takes a bit of luck to stumble across them.

*After less than 1km the road heads downhill for 600m; turn to the left and follow the road; after about 0.5km the trail winds down to the inlet of Mġarr ix-Xini.*

This is the perfect place for a rest and ideal for a picnic, and there is also the enticing prospect of a swim in the cool safe water.

*From Mġarr ix-Xini it is 1.5km uphill along a surfaced road to a T-junction where the road to the right goes to Xewkija and the left road is signposted to Victoria. (Along this road to the left there is a bus stop with a service that will take you back to Victoria).*

**Distance**
4km

**Time**
2 hours

**Start point**
Sannat
✚ 82C2
🚌 50

**End point**
Just north of Mġarr ix-Xini
✚ 83D2
🚌 42,43

**Lunch**
Chip and Dale Bar (£)
✉ Town Square, Victoria
☎ 21560506

*Prickly pears in the foreground of the spectacular church at Xewkija*

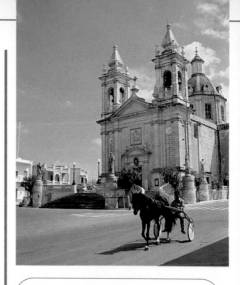

*The relaxed, enviable pace of a Gozitan passing the church in Sannat*

## Did you know ?

*The Maltese falcon, or the Mediterranean peregrine falcon, used to nest under the Ta'Cenc cliffs and at San Dimitri Point on Gozo. Sadly, placed under protection too late, it became extinct in the Maltese islands in the mid-1980s, as did the Mediterranean sea eagle, due to hunting, trapping and egg-collecting. Millions of migrating songbirds are hunted and killed every year.*

 82C2
⊠ 1.5km south of Victoria
🍴 Il-Carruba Restaurant in the Ta'Cenc Hotel (££)
🚌 50, 51 from Victoria
♿ Few
↔ Victoria (▶ 82–85)

### SANNAT ● ●

The village of Sannat, just south of Victoria, has a reputation for lace-making and boasts a fine early 18th-century church, but the best reason for coming here is to begin a walk in the neighbouring plateau of Ta'Cenc. Gozo's top hotel (▶ 103) is also located in Ta'Cenc and to the east of it a track leads to the small harbour of Mġarr-ix-Xini. One could also walk west of Sannat to Xlendi via Munxar.

📮 82B3
⊠ 2.5km northwest of Victoria
☎ 556992
♿ Few
❓ Multilingual information telephones are available

### TA'PINU ●

This imposing basilica, built between 1920 and 1931, hardly blends in with the surrounding countryside but it is an impressive sight nonetheless. There was a chapel on the site from the 16th century, which was named after a Pinu Gauci who spent his time and money repairing it in the 1670s. At the end of the 19th century a local woman claimed to hear a voice in the church and gradually it acquired such a reputation for miracles that a bigger church was built around the original, which can be still seen inside behind the apse.

## XAGĦRA ✪✪

The area around this small town has a number of archaeological sites, the most famous of which is Ġgantija, but Xagħra is worth a visit in its own right. The delightful town square is home to the attractive Church of the Nativity and near by is Ta'Kola, an old windmill still in working order. Also in Xagħra is a **Toy Museum** (✉ 10 Gnien Xibla Street), and **Xerri's Grotto** in Gnien Imrik Street. The 2km route from Xagħra to Calypso's Cave is well signposted but the trip is sadly disappointing because a dark hole in the cliff does not accord with anyone's idea of the site of Odysseus' seven-year abode with Calypso. What is worthwhile is the walk here from the east of Xagħra along a footpath through the lush Ramla valley.

🚩 82C3
✉ 3km east of Victoria
🍴 Café (£), restaurant (➤ 99)
🚌 64, 65 from Victoria
↔ Ġgantija (➤ 16)

**Toy Museum**
☎ 21562489
🕐 Apr, Thu–Sat 10–1; May to mid-Oct, Mon–Sat 10–12, 3–6; Nov–Mar, Sat 10–1
💷 Inexpensive

**Xerri's Grotto**
☎ 560572  🕐 Daily 9–6
💷 Inexpensive

## XEWKIJA ✪✪

The people of this ancient village decided to build a larger church, now known as the Rotunda Church, and for the next 27 years money and labour from the villagers alone fed the construction of a massive edifice that is out of all proportion to the size of the village, and even to Gozo itself. The spectacular dome, which is only comparable to St Peter's in Rome and St Paul's in London, is 75m high and 28m in diameter.

🚩 82C2
✉ 2km southeast of Victoria
🍴 Nearest restaurants are in Victoria
🚌 42 or 43 from Victoria
♿ Few

## XLENDI ✪✪

Xlendi was a little fishing village until discerning visitors in search of relaxation discovered the place. It is still a charming spot, with a children-friendly swimming area which can be supervised while enjoying a drink or a meal (see picture below). There is a diving school, accommodation (➤ 103) and some neat little bars and restaurants facing the sea.

🚩 82B2
✉ 3km southwest of Victoria
🍴 Cafés and restaurants (£–££)
🚌 87 from Victoria
♿ Few
↔ Victoria (➤ 82) Sannat (➤ 88)

*Fresh seafood, alfresco, at Xlendi in true Mediterranean fashion*

89

# A Drive Around Gozo

**Distance**
12km

**Time**
2–5 hours depending on visits

**Start point**
Mgarr ferry terminal
✠ 83D2

**End point**
Dwejra
✠ 82A3

**Lunch**
Il-Kartell (£–££)
✉ Waterfront in Marsalforn
☎ 21556918

**The Kelinu Grima
Maritime Museum**
✉ Parish Priest Street,
Nadur
☎ 21565226
🕐 Mon–Sat 9–4:45 (except
public holidays)

The northern coast of Gozo can be breezy and was once desolate – a place of legends.

*After disembarking at Mġarr follow the signposted road to the right for Nadur. The uphill road leads to a T-junction; take the right turn for Qala, less than 1km away. Exposed Qala has remnants of windmills, sun-baked dwellings and dusty roads with a Moorish feel. Continue straight past the church. Go left at the T-Junction, signposted for Nadur.*

At Nadur there is a maritime museum with exhibits from sailing ships and battleships of World War II.

*Leave Nadur on the road to Victoria and after 1.5km take the right turn at the junction for Xagħra. Follow the signs for Xagħra and follow the road as it climbs uphill with a sign on the right for Ġgantija (➤ 16). Stay on the road to Xagħra after Ġgantija but take the second turning on the right, passing down the side of the church (cafés and bars in the square) and bear left at the signposted junctions for Marsalforn.*

There is a good view of Marsalforn as you enter the village through this backdoor approach. Stop here for lunch and a walk.

*Take the road to Victoria from Marsalforn but turn right at the main junction before entering Victoria and look for the sign to Ta' Pinu (➤ 88).*

The basilica at Ta'Pinu, a centre of pilgrimage for both Gozitans and Maltese, is noted for its mysterious voices and miraculous cures.

*Statues outside the church of Ta'Pinu on the southern coast of Gozo*

*After the short detour to Ta'Pinu, return to the main road and take the signposted left turn for Dwejra. At St Lawrenz bear left in front of the church; the Azure Window is 1km (➤ 86).*

# Where To...

Above: *Gozo boat*
Right: *Automobile Association sign, Valletta*

# Malta

## Prices

Approximate prices for a three-course meal for one without drinks and service:

£ = under LM6
££ = LM6–12
£££ = above LM12

## Fresh Bread

If you are up at around six in the morning you may hear the loud honking of the bread delivery van announcing its arrival in a street. The Maltese take their bread (*hobza*) seriously and in villages there are often two deliveries a day. Be sure to buy your loaf before 11AM.

## Valletta and Floriana

### Blue Room (££–£££)

Just by the palace, this is one of the best Chinese restaurants in Malta. The menu includes a number of set meals and house specials include beef in black pepper and bean curd with minced pork.

✉ 59 Republic Street, Valletta ☎ 21238014 ◉ Tue–Sat 12–3, 7–11

### Café Jubilee (£)

This is a popular bistro decked out in 1920/30s style. The daily specials are recommended, though there is a menu of standard pasta and salad dishes.

✉ 125 St Lucy Street, Valletta ☎ 21252332 ◉ Daily 8–1AM

### Café Marquee (£)

There are tables inside, but only the weather keeps people away from the out-door tables facing St John's Co-Cathedral. No surprises with the food: pizzas, burgers, pastas, salads, sandwiches and ice-cream.

✉ 9 St John's Square, Valletta ☎ 21236257 ◉ Daily 9–7

### Café Premier (£)

Outdoor tables in Republic Square, ideal for people-watching, and a musty interior that looks unchanged from decades ago. Set meals, pizzas, pasta, burgers, lots of drinks and a fairly good vegetarian salad.

✉ Republic Square, Valletta ☎ 21247300 ◉ Daily 8:30–5:30

### Cocopazzo (£)

Cocopazzo is a neat, cultured little restaurant, suitable for lunch or dinner, away from the noise of Republic Street. The Mediterranean food is mostly salads, pasta, chicken and especially fish dishes. Pleasant service.

✉ Valletta Buildings, South Street ☎ 21235706 ◉ Mon–Fri 9–3, 6:30–10, Sat–Sun 12–3, 6:30–10

### Eddie's Café Regina (£)

The interior is brightly lit but the tables outside in Republic Square are even more brightly lit on a warm Mediterranean morning. Pizzas, pastas, grills, milkshakes and one or two Maltese dishes, including *qarabali* (stuffed marrows). Easily distinguished from the other cafés in the square by the green colour of the tables and waiters' uniforms.

✉ Republic Square, Valletta ☎ 21246454 ◉ Daily 10–10

### De Lucia (£)

An unpretentious little café, handy for the Museum of Fine Arts in the same street, serving excellent caper and bean salads, light snacks and good coffee. Newspapers are available.

✉ 28a South Street, Valletta ☎ 21236258 ◉ Mon–Fri 8–8, Sat 8–1PM. Closed Sun

### Da Pippo (££)

Da Pippo has also been discovered by discerning Maltese to judge by the stream of locals popping in for lunch. The menu of Italian and Maltese dishes should satisfy most tastes.

✉ 136 Melita Street ☎ 21248029 ◉ Mon–Sat 11:30–3:30

### De Robertis Restaurant (£££)

Dine out on the terrace of the 16th-century former Palazzo Xara, one of the finest up-market addresses on the island. Good Mediterranean and French cuisine and attentive service.

✉ **Castille Hotel, St Paul's Street, Valletta** ☎ 21220173 ⊙ **Daily 12–2:30, 7–10**

### Scalini (££)

A small Italian menu with mostly meat dishes, for example *scalloppini ai funghi*. The interior is pleasantly cool and unpretentious.

✉ **320 South Street (opposite the Museum of Fine Arts), Valletta** ☎ 21246221 ⊙ **Mon–Fri 12–2:30, 7–11, Sat 7–11**

## Around Malta

### Balzan
#### Corinthia Room Restaurant (£££)

The main restaurant of the Corinthia Palace Hotel and one of the best in Malta. The setting is superb. There is one central dining area with the surrounding rooms of the villa forming dining adjuncts. The whole place is elegantly furnished and decorated in a grand style. European menu.

✉ **Corinthia Palace Hotel, De Paule Avenue, Attard** ☎ 21440801 ⊙ **Daily 7PM–10PM; also lunch 12:30–2:30 Sun** 🚌 40

### Buġibba
#### Chez Gaetane (££

Always the subject of good reviews for its friendly service and value for money, Chez Gaetane is an excellent family option, with a Maltese and Continental menu.

✉ **79 St Anthony Street, Bay Square, Buġibba** ☎ 21574453 ⊙ **Mon–Sat 11–11**

### Granny's (£)

Recommended by a reader for its value-for-money breakfasts, Granny's serves equally satisfying lunches and dinners and the price of drinks is another reason to call in. Just off Buġibba's main square.

✉ **Pioneer Road** ☎ 21378460 ⊙ **Mon–Sun 9AM–11PM**

### La Stalla (£–££)

Recommended for its range of pizzas and pastas at reasonable prices, La Stalla also offers steaks and seafood, plus a traditional English roast on Sunday.

✉ **Triq It-Turisti, Buġibba** ☎ 21491240 ⊙ **Mon–Sat 7–11**

## Dingli Cliffs
### Bobbyland Bar and Restaurant (£)

A landmark restaurant which is not easily missed if you turn to the right after arriving at Dingli Cliffs from Rabat. At weekends in the summer the tables are oversubscribed and there can be an air of frenzy about the place. Come at a quieter time and the view out to sea will overwhelm. The food is usually excellent, with an emphasis on traditional meat dishes featuring rabbit and lamb, but the fish is always a welcome alternative.

✉ **Panoramic Road, Dingli Cliffs** ☎ 21452895 ⊙ **Tue–Fri 11:30–2:30, 7–10:30, Sat 11:30–2, 7–10:30, Sun 11:30–2:15, 7–10** 🚌 81

## Marsaskala
### Al Kafe (£)

A pleasant *pizzeria* and cafeteria with a prime location on the waterfront and tables filling the pavement under giant umbrellas. There is a pub a few doors down, Summer Nights, which is under the same management, and there is also a guest house.

✉ **Marina Street, Marsaskala** ☎ 21822528 ⊙ **Wed–Mon 8AM–11PM** 🚌 19, 22

### A Fish Dictionary

| MALTESE | ENGLISH |
| --- | --- |
| *acciola* | amberjack |
| *cerna* | grouper |
| *dorado* | swordfish |
| *dott* | stone bass |
| *klamer* | squid |
| *pagru* | sea bream |
| *san pietro* | john dory |
| *pesce sicca* | cuttlefish |

### Pastizzi
The traditional Maltese snack is sometimes translated as cheesecake but this can be misleading. They are in fact made from a rich flaky pastry and a savoury filling of ricotta cheese or dried peas. They are eaten mid-morning or mid-afternoon with tea and coffee. High in calories but friendly to the taste buds.

### Double Dutch (£)
Situated on the quiet side of the bay, this busy bar serves a range of tasty snacks to accompany the cold beer.

✉ Triq Is-Salini
☎ 99297235 🕐 Mon–Sun 10–2:30, 5–midnight 🚌 19, 20

### Grabiel (££)
Probably the most popular restaurant with local people and deservedly so because the prices are reasonable and the food is very good. There is a wide range of starters and while the main dishes are mostly meat the counter is usually overflowing with examples of the locally caught fresh fish. The restaurant is right in the centre of town. Recommended.

✉ Mifsud Bonnici Square
☎ 21684194
🕐 Mon–Sat noon–2, 5–midnight. Closed 14–28 Aug
🚌 19, 22

### Jakarta (££)
A small but smart interior with white linen tablecloths and a menu of oriental dishes. There is a set meal for two people besides the à la carte choices which include satay, spare-ribs and crispy duck with pancakes. There is a string of cheaper places to eat between Jakarta and Sun City (► 109)

✉ 117 Dun Tarcis Agius Square
☎ 21639452 🕐 Tue–Sun 7–11, Sun noon–2PM 🚌 19, 20

### Tal-Familja (££)
Past the Sun City cinema, this is a large restaurant with outdoor tables available. The fish and local dishes are likely to be the best items on the menu and vegetarians catered for.

✉ Triq-il-Gardiel
☎ 21632161
🕐 Tue–Sun 12–5, 6:30–2AM

## Marsaxlokk
### Hunter's Tower (££)
This restaurant has been in operation for over 30 years and has grown into a large operation with plenty of space in the main dining room and the shady garden. The menu concentrates on fresh fish, but is augmented by pizzas and Maltese dishes.

✉ Wilga Street ☎ 21651792
🕐 Tue–Thu 11:30–3, Fri–Sun 6:30–11, 21 Sep–21 Jun; Tue–Thu 6:30–11, Fri–Sun 11:30–3, 6:30–11, 22 Jun–20 Sep

### Ir-Rizzu (££)
This is an excellent fish restaurant and it is easily found on the sea front in Marsaxlokk. Meat dishes are available but locals wax lyrical about the variety of fish available and the unerring skill with which it is prepared for the table. This is partly because the traditional Maltese method of steaming fish is used here.

✉ Xatt is-Sjjieda ☎ 21871569
🕐 Daily 12–3, 6:30–10:30
🚌 27 from Valletta, 427 from Buġibba, 627 from Paceville

### Is-Sajjied Bar & Restaurant (££)
Great views of the sea, which is where the best dishes on the restaurant's menu are caught. There are other Italian-style dishes available but it's the local fish that make Is-Sajjied a rather special place for lunch or dinner.

✉ Xatt Is-Sajjieda
☎ 21652549 🕐 Tue–Sun 12–2:30, 7–10:30 (closed for dinner on Sun; closed for lunch on Sat) 🚌 19, 22

## Mdina and Rabat
### Bacchus (££)
The bare stone walls of this restaurant once housed Mdina's store of gunpowder but, notwithstanding a

dungeon-like atmosphere, this is one of the best places for a decent meal in Mdina. There are some tasty *hors d'oeuvres*, speciality fish dishes, soups, grills and pasta; the Grand Opera dessert will have you singing.

✉ Inguanez Street, Mdina
☎ 21454981 ⏰ Daily 9–9
🚍 80, 81 from Valletta, 65 from Sliema

## Ciappetti Tea Rooms (££)

Lovely courtyard setting with wooden tables and a simple short menu of salads, rolls and home-made cakes. There is an open-air terrace upstairs on the bastion.

✉ 5 St Agatha's Esplanade, Mdina ☎ 21459987 ⏰ Daily 11–3:30, 7:30–11 🚍 80, 81 from Valletta, 65 from Sliema

## Cuckoo's Nest Tavern (£)

This is one of the tiniest restaurants in Malta with three tables and a diminutive bar, but it has character. Nearly all dishes on the menu are meat, featuring beef and lamb.

✉ 9 St Paul Street, Rabat
☎ 21455946 ⏰ Daily 11:30–2:30, 7–10 🚍 80, 81, 83, 84 from Valletta, 65 from Sliema, 86 from Buġibba

## The Medina (£££)

Located inside an old Norman dwelling, with a vine-laden courtyard for summer meals and a comfortable interior with a fire burning in winter. The food is French, with Italian and Maltese influences here and there. Can be quite romantic.

✉ 7 Holy Cross Street, Mdina
☎ 21454004 ⏰ Mon–Sat 7:30PM–10:30 (closed on public holidays) 🚍 80, 81, 83, 84 from Valletta, 65 from Sliema, 86 from Buġibba

## De Mondion (£££)

Enjoy a cocktail downstairs in the hotel's grand sitting room before heading upstairs to the open-air terrace where a table is best reserved in advance to ensure a panoramic view of the landscape, dominated by Mosta's dome. Fine mediterranean cuisine and starters like avocado pear in coriander and tarragon batter served with Aragula and an olive tapenade.

✉ Xara Palace Hotel, Misrah il-Kunsill, Mdina ☎ 21450560 ⏰ 7:30–10:30 🚍 80, 84 from Valletta, 65 from Sliema

## Fontanella Tea Garden (£)

Panoramic view from the tables of the battlements of Mdina. Only light meals like sandwiches and salads but an excellent selection of homemade cakes – lemon meringue, black forest gateau. Recommended.

✉ 1 Bastion Street, Mdina
☎ 21454264 ⏰ Summer, daily 10–10; winter, daily 10–6 🚍 80, 81 from Valletta, 65 from Sliema

## SB Grotto Tavern (£–££)

Step down, literally rather than metaphorically, into this terrific little tavern serving some real surprises. Fondue and moules mariniere on the menu and an above-average wine list.

✉ Parish Square, Rabat
☎ 21455138 ⏰ Daily 12–2:15, 7–10

## Point de Vue (£–££)

Located just outside Mdina Gate, this is a tourist restaurant with menus in English, French and German. There are outdoor and inside tables and some of the Maltese dishes make a refreshing change. (The French and German menus carry more Maltese meals than the English one – a management decision no doubt based on experience).

### *Fenek biz–zalza*

Rabbit has been eaten in Malta for as long as anyone can remember and in rabbit stew (*fenek biz-zalza*) the taste has been perfected. The rabbit is fried in a mixture of red wine and fat and then stewed slowly with vegetables, herbs and more wine. Sometimes the rabbit is roasted or served inside a pie along with vegetables and pieces of pork – *torta tal-fenek*.

## Sweet Desserts

The British influence may account for the puddings but Italy must be thanked for the *gelaterias* (ice-cream parlours) and Sicily is regarded as the source of *kannoli*, a dessert that is worth seeking out. It comprises cornets of deep-fried pastry filled with ricotta cheese and sweetened with chocolate.

**A Maltese Picnic**
Glorious weather invites a picnic so prepare *hobz biz–zejt* (bread with oil) or purchase it at a coffee shop. Traditionally the farmer's packed lunch, thick bread is dipped in olive oil then spread with pulped tomato before being heaped with olives, capers, garlic, vinegar and salt and pepper.

Try the *haruf imsajjar fl-imbio* (spicy marinated lamb in wine), which appears on all the menus. There are also inexpensive set meals.

5 The Saqqajja, Rabat 21454117 Daily 9–11:30 80, 81, 83, 84 from Valletta, 65 from Sliema, 86 from Buġibba

**Trattoria AD 1530 (££)**
Cosy dining room in the vaulted chambers of the Xara Place Hotel or in the historic piazza, with the same stylish service as the De Mondion (➤ 95), but a lighter menu of excellent pasta dishes and salads.

Xara Palace Hotel, Misrah il-Kunsill, Mdina 21450560 Daily 10:30AM–11PM (closed Tue evening in winter) 80, 84 from Valletta, 65 from Sliema

## Mellieħa
### Alantil Bay Restaurant (£)
This family-run bar and restaurant serves snacks, grills, salads and burgers. No surprises with the food except for a couple of Maltese dishes like rabbit and *bragioli* (rolled sliced beef filled with ham), but it is inexpensive and reliable and there are outside tables.

61 G Borg Oliver Street, Mellieħa 21573049 Daily 10–1PM 43, 44, 45 from Valletta, 48 from Buġibba and Ċirkewwa, 645 from Sliema and Ċirkewwa

### The Arches (£££)
Centrally located on the main street, The Arches restaurant has long been considered one of the best in Malta. It has a good wine list and the European cuisine is complemented by mouth-watering desserts.

113 Borg Oliver Street 21523460 Mon–Sat 7–10:30 43, 44, 45 from Valletta, 48 from Buġibba and Ċirkewwa, 645 from Sliema and Ċirkewwa

### Giuseppi's Wine Bar (££–£££)
The menu changes according to the season so expect something fresh with the occasional surprise; the daily specials are good value and fresh fish is nearly always available.

25 St Helen Street, Mellieħa 21574882 Tue–Sun 7:30–11 43, 44, 45 from Valletta, 48 from Buġibba and Ċirkewwa, 645 from Sliema and Ċirkewwa

### Half Way Inn (£–££)
As the name suggests, halfway down a hill between the village and the beach. Recommended by a reader for its generous portions, fresh fish and Maltese dishes. Popular with locals and visitors.

Marfa Road, Mellieħa 21573a Bay 21521637 Daily 6–12 43–45 from Valletta, 48 from Buġibba and Ċirkewwa, 645 from Sliema and Ċirkewwa

## St Julian's, Paceville and St George's Bay
### The Avenue (££)
There is no mistaking the popularity of The Avenue, a gem of a place in an area not noted for quality cuisine. People come here for the big portions of good value, tasty food: pasta, pizza, burgers, meat, fish, salads, grills.

Gort Street, Paceville 21311753 Mon–Sun 12–2:30, 6–11:30 (closed for lunch on Sunday) 62, 64–68, 70, 627, 645, 652, 662, 667, 671

### Barracuda (££)
The original beams of an 18th-century residence still support this waterfront restaurant. The food is Italian but the speciality is always the fresh fish, cooked whole.

194 Main Street, St Julian's 21331817 7–10:30. Closed Sun in winter 62, 64,

### Le Bistro (££)

Situated at lobby level in the Radisson SAS Hotel, Le Bistro is worth keeping in mind as one of the very few 24-hour food and drink places of any quality on the island. For fine dining go down the marble staircase to Le Petillant (£££).

🏠 **Radisson SAS Hotel, St George's Bay** ☎ **21374894**
🕐 **24 hours** 🚌 **62, 64, 65, 67, 68, 70**

### Caffe Raffael (£)

Pizza, pasta, salads and kebabs in a lovely stone-built restaurant. Reserve an outdoor waterfront table. Deservedly busy.

🏠 **St George's Road, St Julian's** ☎ **21332000** 🕐 **Daily 10–11**
🚌 **62, 64, 65, 67, 68, 70**

### Eastern Breeze (£££)

Asian fusion at its finest, Eastern Breeze is a contender for the best restaurant in Malta. Everything works, from the service to the food to the neat, Jacobsen-like cutlery, and the sizzling hot chocolate dessert caps it all.

🏠 **Intercontinental Hotel, St George's Bay, St Julian's** ☎ **21377600** 🕐 **Tue–Sat 7–11**
🚌 **62, 64, 65, 67, 68, 70**

### La Maltija (££)

The best for Maltese food, with suitably rustic decor. Starters include *aljotta* (fish soup) and spaghetti with rabbit sauce. Mains include *bragioli* (rolled sliced beef with ham), stuffed marrows and swordfish.

🏠 **1 Church Street, Paceville** ☎ **21339602** 🕐 **Mon–Sat 6–11**
🚌 **62, 64–68**

### Peppino's (££–£££)

At lunchtime only the wine bar area is open for pasta and salads, but during the evening the top two floors have tables overlooking the bay and reservations are essential at weekends, especially for the top terrace, which has a superb view. There is a good wine list.

🏠 **31 St George's Road, St Julian's** ☎ **21373200**
🕐 **Mon–Sat 12–2:30, 7–11**
🚌 **62, 64–68**

### Piccolo Padre Pizeria (£)

Situated below the Barracuda restaurant in the same old building; as well as pizzas (try the pizzotto) there are pasta dishes and pleasant starters.

🏠 **194 Main Street, St Julian's** ☎ **21344875** 🕐 **Daily 6:30–11:30**

### The Plough and Anchor (££)

An insistent nautical theme in this popular restaurant where breaded scampi, steaks, prawns, chicken and pasta dishes are firm favourites with returning customers. Children are welcome.

🏠 **1 Main Street, St Julian's** ☎ **21334725** 🕐 **Tue–Sun 12–2, 6:30–10:30 (closed for a week from Easter Monday and last week of July)**

### Quadro (£££)

Fine dining indoors or outside under the stars. Starters like smoked salmon and cavroux cheese and main courses like monkfish and cuttlefish with a potato tart cooked in the ink of the fish. Quality service.

🏠 **Westin Dragonara Resort, St Julian's** ☎ **21381000**
🕐 **Mon–Sat 12:30–2:30, daily 7:30–11** 🚌 **62, 64, 65, 67, 68, 70**

### Zen (££–£££)

This smart location is the perfect place for a modern Japanese restaurant and Zen serves excellent fresh sushi

### Delicious and Different

Look for *bigilla*, a dish served with toasted bread that originated during the privations of World War II when there was little choice of food. Mashed beans are mixed with a pumpkin sauce to make this delicious repast. Cumin and garlic give it a spicy taste. Served at the Barracuda in St Julian's (► left).

**A Cheese with Attitude**
Imported cheeses from Italy are readily available but it would be a pity to miss out on *gbejna*. This cheese made from goat's milk is now made in Malta but it is best enjoyed in Gozo, from where it originates. The peppered version (*tal-bzar*) is far tastier than the unpeppered.

and sashimi, plus a range of other delicate dishes.
✉ Portomaso Marina, St Julian's ☎ 21386500
🕐 Daily 7–11

## St Paul's Bay
### Gillieru Restaurant (££–£££)
A well-established and renowned restaurant with a seafront location; reserve one of the outside tables. The menu is mainly seafood and the freshly caught fish is also used for Maltese dishes like *klamar mimli* (stuffed squid with egg, olives, anchovies and tomatoes). A 15 per cent discount for hotel residents.
✉ 66 Church Street, St Paul's Bay ☎ 21573480 🕐 Daily 12:15–2:30, 7:30–11 (bar open 10AM–midnight) 🚌 43, 44, 45, 49, 50 from Valletta, 48 from Ċirkewwa

### Misfits (££)
The chef is French but it's the authentic Maltese dishes on the menu, like rabbit stewed in garlic and wine, that make a foray into the teenage jungle of Paceville worth while.
✉ Paceville Avenue, St Julians ☎ 21331766 🕐 6:30PM–11:30 🚌 62, 64–66, 68, 70, 627, 645, 652, 662, 667, 671

### Nostalgia (££–£££)
The historic setting of a stone-vaulted chamber is matched by the French and Italian cuisine at this atmospheric restaurant. The owner/chef ensures the highest standards.
✉ 14 Mosta Road, St Paul's Bay ☎ 21584866 🕐 Dinner daily, lunch Sun 🚌 43, 44, 45, 49, 50 from Valletta

### Porto del Sol (££)
The chef is French but it's the authentic Maltese dishes on the menu, like rabbit stewed in garlic and wine, that make a foray into the

teenage jungle of Paceville worth while.
✉ Paceville Avenue, St Julians ☎ 21331766 🕐 6:30PM–11:30 🚌 62, 64–66, 68, 70, 627, 645, 652, 662, 667, 671

## Sliema
### La Cuccagna (£)
At the sea end of Amery Street, this quaint and cosy little place can be relied on for tasty homemade pizza and pasta dishes; the starters and desserts are good as well.
✉ 47 Amery Street, Sliema ☎ 21346703 🕐 Tue–Sat 7–midnight

### Il Merill (££)
This family-run restaurant offers a combination of local Maltese cuisine and standard international dishes. It's the place to try something different – the proprietor will be happy to advise.
✉ 9 St Vincent Street, Sliema ☎ 21332172 🕐 Mon–Sat 7–10:30

### Snoopy's Restaurant & Bar (£–££)
Snoopy's is a reliable stop for snacks or meals throughout the day. It's particularly popular in the evenings. Good 'bar-meal' style food.
✉ 265 Tower Road, Sliema ☎ 21345466 🕐 Daily 11AM–midnight

## Vittoriosa
### Café Riche (£)
Easy to find, being on the right just before entering Vittoriosa's Gate of Provence. Opened in 1933 as a dance hall, there are artefacts hanging about the walls and ceiling which evoke a sense of history. Only snacks like toasted sandwiches – though on Tuesdays *hobs bizejt* (a local bread) is available – but this is the only place to enjoy a bite of food so close to Vittoriosa.

☒ Cospicua ☏ 21820989
◎ Mon–Sat 10–4, Sun 10–1

# Gozo

### Churchill (£–££)

Overlooking the sea and with tables by the water's edge, a lunch here could easily turn into a lazy afternoon. There is a separate evening menu and a bar that stays open until the last person leaves.

☒ Marina Street, Xlendi
☏ 21555614 ◎ Mon–Sun
10–late

### Gesther (££)

A family-owned traditional eatery serving excellent, simple Gozitan dishes, including locally sourced cheeses and meats. Try the rabbit in tomato sauce – mouthwatering!

☒ 8 September Avenue, Xagħra
☏ 21556621 ◎ Mon–Sat
12–2:30 🚌 42, 43

### Il-Kartell (£–££)

A lively waterside restaurant with a good reputation for fresh fish. There is a helpful explanation on a notice board of the various types of local fish. A speciality is mixed seafood with cream, but assorted pizzas are also available. Musical entertainment is performed at night.

☒ Main Street, Marsalforn
☏ 21556918 ◎ Thu–Tue
11:30–3:30, 7–10:30 (Closed
weekdays Nov–Jan) 🚌 21 from
Victoria

### Il-Tmun (££–£££)

Near the centre of town in a quiet street, with tables on the pavement as well as inside. The food is Mediterranean along with some Maltese dishes; the best place for fine food in Xlendi.

☒ 3 Mt Carmel Street, Xlendi
☏ 21581787 ◎ Wed–Mon
12–3, 6:30–10 (Closed Tue–Thu in
Jan, most of Dec and Feb)

### Jeffrey's (££)

A modest and friendly restaurant, with a small open-air section at the back. The food is delicious, and while the menu follows what is locally available at the time, visitors may depend on fish, rabbit and pasta.

☒ 10 Triq l-Gharb ☏ 21561006
◎ Mon–Sat 7–10. Closed
Nov–Mar 🚌 2, 91 from Victoria

### Oleander (££)

A cosy little family–run restaurant, surrounded by oleanders, serving delicious Maltese favourites.

☒ 10 Victory Square
☏ 21557230 ◎ Tue–Sun
11:30–3, 6:30–10

### Tatitas Restaurant (££)

An excellent 'price versus service' option in the west of the island. Typical friendly Gozitan service; local and international dishes.

☒ San Lawrenz Swuare, San
Lawrenz ☏ 21565099
◎ Lunch daily 12–2:30, Mar to
mid-Jul; dinner daily 6–10:30,
Mar–Oct

### Trattoria (££)

For a more formal dining experience there is the L'Ortolan downstarirs, but the Trattoria is pleasingly informal. Tables indoor and out, a diverse menu that caters for vegetarians, and fresh herbs from the hotel's gardens.

☒ Kempinski Hotel, San
Lawrenz ☏ 22115620
◎ Daily 6:30–11

### Stuffed Delights

Stuffed dishes are common in Maltese cuisine. Octopus, squid and cuttlefish are all stuffed, as are aubergines, marrows and peppers. Vegetarians should ask for stuffed vegetables without mincemeat for this is often added to the onions, tomatoes, herbs and breadcrumbs that make up the filling.

# Malta

**Prices**
Expect to pay for a double room per night in summer:

| | |
|---|---|
| **£** | = under LM20 |
| **££** | = LM20–40 |
| **£££** | = over LM40 |

**Accommodation Online**
All accommodation available in Malta can be checked out at www.visitmalta.com Accommodation can be booked online at www.hotelinfomalta.com

## Valletta

### British Hotel (£–££)
The longest established hotel in Valletta has a lovely situation overlooking the Grand Harbour. All 44 rooms on six floors have *en suite* facilities and telephone, and some have balconies. A rooftop sundeck for sun bathing and drinks and an inexpensive restaurant compensate for the narrow corridors and stairs.
www.britishhotel.com
📧 40 Battery Street, Valletta
☎ 21239022

### Grand Harbour Hotel (£)
A superb location with outstanding views of the Grand Harbour and an inexpensive restaurant. The rooms can be small and facilities are basic but nevertheless this still represents value for money.
www.grandharbourhotel.com
📧 47 Battery Street, Valletta
☎ 21246003

### Hotel Osborne (££)
Recommended by a reader, the Osborne is a smart place to have a room if staying in Valletta. It has an air of elegance, a pleasant dining room, a bar and a lounge area. Popular with British and German visitors.
www.osbornehotel.com
📧 50 South Street, Valletta
☎ 21232127;

## Around Malta

### Balzan

#### Corinthia Palace Hotel (£££)
One of the top hotels in Malta. The rooms have everything from fax points to hair dryers and the hotel's health spa is state-of-the-art

with sauna, massage, gym, mudstream baths, aromatherapy and reflexology. Indoor and outdoor pools and tennis and squash courts complete the fitness facilities. There is also a courtesy bus to Valletta.
www.corinthiahotels.com
📧 De Paule Av, Balzan
☎ 21440301 📠 40

### Marsaskala

#### Charian Hotel (£)
A friendly, family-owned hotel, close to the centre of town. All the rooms have en-suite shower and toilet, and there's a heated Jacuzzi on the rooftop garden.
www.charianhotel.com
📧 Salini Road, Marsaskala
☎ 21636392

### Rabat

#### Point de Vue (£)
This family-run budget guesthouse is in a 17th-century building and apparently guests have been staying here since 1898. The location is central, just outside Mdina Gate, and some of the rooms can offer a balcony as well as picturesque views of the surrounding Maltese countryside.
www.pointdevuemalta.com
📧 5 Saqqaja Square, Rabat
☎ 21454117 📠 80, 81, 83, 84, 86, 65

### Mellieħa

#### Luna Holiday Complex (££)
Self-catering apartments in a modern complex with a pool, sun terrace, bar, restaurant, fitness room and mini-market. Bus stop is near by and it's only a short walk to the beach. Studios, sleeping up to three, plus one- and two-bedroomed apartments

are available; May to October and minimum three-day stay.

www.searchmalta.com/luna

📧 **Marfa Road, Mellieħa Bay**
📞 21521645; 🚌 44, 45 from Valletta, 48 from Buġibba and Ċirkewwa, 645 from Sliema and Ċirkewwa

### Mellieħa Holiday Centre (££)

This Danish-run complex comprises 150 self-catering bungalows, each with two bedrooms, Olympic-sized swimming pool, restaurant, bar, playground and supermarket. The bungalow tariff is reasonable and in winter enters the budget category.

📧 **Mellieħa Bay** 📞 21573900; dff@vol.net.mt 🚌 43

## St Julian's, Paceville and St George's Bay

### Corinthia San Gorg (£££)

The St George's Bay area is being developed as an accommodation centre and the San Gorg holds pride of place. All 250 rooms on the six floors have a balcony and sea view. The water facilities are first class and there are health and fitness facilities.

www.corinthiahotels.com

📧 **St George's Bay, St Julian's**
📞 21374114 🚌 62, 64, 65, 67, 68, 70

### Hotel Juliani (£££)

Overlooking the harbour of St Julian's, this 4-star boutique hotel is a converted town house with 21st-century upgrades to its décor and modern deco in its 44 rooms. It's one of the hippest places on the island.

www.hoteljuliani.com

📧 **12 St George's Road, St Julian's** 📞 21388000 🚌 61, 62, 64, 67, 68 from Valletta, 70, 86 from Buġibba

### St George's Park Complex (££)

With over 800 beds, there is quite a range of rooms, studios and apartments. During the winter, groups stay here for as long as three months at a time. The hotel's lido has two pools and there is a good leisure centre with squash courts, sauna and gym. Certainly not everyone's cup of tea and definitely not a place for quiet relaxation.

www.sgp.com.mt

📧 **St Julian's** 📞 21351146 🚌 62, 64, 65, 67, 68, 70

### La Vallette Resort (£££)

An all-round resort that welcomes families and with a host of facilities – pools for adults and children and a heated indoor one for winter, gym, squash courts – as well as five bars and a restaurant.

www.sgp.com.mt

📧 **Dragonara Road, St Julian's** 📞 21351147

### Villa Rosa (££)

This brightly coloured hotel seems quite homely compared to the new giant hotel blocks that are gradually dominating the area. For a lot less money than those, the Villa Rosa offers indoor and outdoor pools, sports, gym and restaurant and easy access to nearby restaurants and also to the dynamic nightlife of Paceville.

📧 **St George's Bay, St Julian's** 📞 21342707 🚌 62, 64, 65, 67, 68, 70

## St Paul's Bay, Buġibba and Qawra

### The Coastline (£££)

Panoramic views of Salina Bay. There is a shuttle bus to and from Buġibba, but this might not be ideal for guests who want lots of late nights where the action is. There is no excuse for not keeping fit here: an excellent gym, sauna, indoor pool and tennis courts are on the premises.

www.coastline.com.mt

### On the Move

Budget-conscious visitors to Malta and Gozo who plan to travel around the islands staying in different hotels and guest houses each night should collect from the tourist office a useful little brochure that lists all one- and two-star hotels, hostels and guest houses and explains the available facilites.

**Staying Put**

Visitors whose stay in Malta does not exceed three months are classified as non-residents. Anyone wishing to stay longer is required to show proof that their income will enable them to live independently in Malta. Temporary residents become subject to local taxes after six months.

✉ **Coast Road, Salina Bay**
☎ **21573781** 🚌 **70, 449, 645, 652 stop outside**

## Primera (£)

Showing its age, a little, but still a comfortable abode in the heart of Buġibba and close to the sea and promenade. Most of the eighty-plus rooms have small balconies and side views of the mediterranean. A heated indoor pool, rooftop terrace, child-friendly.

**www.primerahotel.com**
✉ **Pioneer Road, Bugibba** ☎ **21573880** 🚌 **43, 44, 45, 49, 50 from Valletta, 48 from Ċirkewwa**

## Sea View Hotel (£)

A small pool at the front of the hotel, suitable for children, and adjoining bar. Karaoke sessions twice a week, live music on Friday nights, pool table and internet service. Full- and half-board available; open all year.

✉ **Qawra Road** ☎ **21573105; fax: 581788**

## Sol Suncrest Hotel (£££)

With over 400 rooms, it manages to avoid being impersonal and it has the best facilities of any hotel in the area. There are five restaurants, a disco, two lidos and two outdoor pools, tennis and squash courts, a health centre and a water sports centre. Facilities for people with disabilites are very good.

**www.suncresthotel.com**
✉ **Qawra Coast Road, Qawra** ☎ **21577101** 🚌 **48, 49, 51, 70, 86**

## White Dolphin Residence (£)

Nearly fifty self-catering apartments located on the Qawra seafront. Most of the apartments have balconies overlooking the pool and the smaller Qawra bay. There is a rooftop sundeck area with pool; children are welcome.

**www.whitedolphinmalta.com**
✉ **Qawra Road**
☎ **21577485 (also fax)**

# Sliema

## Hotel Fortina Spa Resort (£££)

The newest and most sophisticated spa resort in Malta offering an all-inclusive package whcih includes daily spa treatments. The hotel has seven swimming pools and seven restaurants to choose from. Main garden area and pool for adults only.

**www.hotelfortina.com**
✉ **Tigne sea front, Sliema** ☎ **23460000** 🚌 **61, 62, 64, 67, 68 from Valletta, 70, 86 from Buġibba, 65, 86 from Rabat, 645 from Ċirkewwa, 652 from Golden Bay**

## Park Hotel (££)

A chic six-storey hotel with modern art and fake marble giving a swank look to the lobby. Restaurant, café, indoor pool, sauna and fitness room. Child-friendly, and half-board available.

**www.parkhotel.com.mt**
✉ **Graham Street** ☎ **21343780** 🚌 **61, 62, 64, 67, 68 from Valletta, 70, 86 from Buġibba, 65, 86 from Rabat, 645 from Ċirkewwa, 652 from Golden Bay**

## Plaza & Plaza Regency Hotel (££)

A prime location on the seafront. All the rooms have air-conditioning, the more expensive a sea view. Good middle-range establishment, classified as a three-star hotel, with a pool and restaurant.

✉ **251 Tower Road**
☎ **21341295;**
**plaza@aghl.com.mt** 🚌 **61, 62, 64, 67, 68 from Valletta, 70, 86 from Buġibba, 65, 86 from Rabat, 645 from Ċirkewwa, 652 from Golden Bay**

## Sliema Chalet Hotel (££)

This is a smart and comfortable hotel overlooking Sliema's

promenade and the big blue Mediterranean; the sunrise is wonderful from the rooftop terrace. There are 50 rooms, some with sea views. A good restaurant, the Café Damier (➤ 52).

www.vol.net.my/com/chalet

✉ 17 Tower Road ☎ 21335575 🚌 61, 62, 64, 67, 68 from Valletta, 70, 86 from Buġibba

### Sliema Hotel (£)

A smart modern hotel with a café that opens out onto the pavement. Rooms with a view of the sea cost more and a range of family rooms are also available.

www.sliemahotel.com ✉ 59 The Strand ☎ 21324886 🚌 61, 62, 64, 67, 68 from Valletta, 70, 86 from Buġibba, 65, 86 from Rabat

## Gozo

### Downtown Hotel (££)

This modern, small, 26-room hotel is situated in the heart of the capital and is perfect for touring Gozo as it is close to the bus station and within walking distance of the city sites. No beach, but there's a roof pool in summer.

www.downtown.com.mt

✉ Triq- i-Ewropa, Victoria ☎ 22108000

### Kempinski San Lawrenz Resort & Spa (£££)

It is hard to beat the location of this five-star hotel; it seems to be camouflaged. Inside, all is splendid luxury and the restaurants are some of the best on the island. Plus pools, squash and tennis courts.

www.kempinski-gozo.com

✉ Triq- il-Rokon, San Lawrenz ☎ 22110000

### Lantern Guesthouse (£)

A family-run B&B situated in the centre of town, with a small restaurant. The Lantern is a very friendly establishment, with a good reputation.

www.mal.net.mt/lantern/

✉ Qbajjar Road, Marsalforn ☎ 21556285 🚌 42, 43 from Victoria

### Marsalforn Guesthouse (£)

Located close to the seafront, its 20 rooms offer economical accommodation. There is a small restaurant. Basic, clean and well-managed.

✉ Rabat Road, Marsalforn ☎ 21556147 🚌 21 from Victoria

### St Patrick's Hotel (£££)

One of the best hotels in Gozo. Most rooms have balconies with views of either the sea, the countryside or a courtyard and there is a restaurant, bar and water sports for guests' use, making this a useful base.

www.vjborg.com/stpatricks

✉ Xlendi ☎ 21562951 🚌 87 from Victoria

### San Antonio (££)

A family-run guesthouse with air-conditioning, a small pool and a restaurant. Good feedback from visitors who have stayed here.

www.clubgozo.com.mt

✉ Tower Street, Xlendi ☎ 21563555 🚌 87 from Victoria

### Ta'Cenc Hotel & Spa (£££)

A strong contender for the best hotel in Malta and Gozo. It is in a tremendous location, overlooking cliffs and sea. All 83 rooms are stylishly decorated and have a terrace or garden. Sporting facilities include tennis courts and swimming pools and there is a private rocky beach with its own restaurant/bar. The accommodation includes stone-built *trulli* bungalows with distictive beehive roofs.

www.vjborg.com/tacenc

✉ Sannat, Gozo ☎ 21556819 🚌 52 from Victoria

### Buying a Property

Non-Maltese visitors can buy and sell most types of property, over a minimum value of LM15,000, after obtaining a permit from the Ministry of Finance (☎ 21236306). Only one property can be owned at any one time and the funds used to buy must be transferred from abroad. Property agents are easy to find, especially in the Sliema area, and *The Times* on Mondays and Thursdays has especially large rental listings.

# Markets

## When and Where

Shops in Malta and Gozo generally open Monday to Friday at 9AM and often close for a couple of hours in the afternoon before re-opening around 4PM and finally closing at 7PM. On Saturday shops are usually only open for the morning, but on Sunday very few open. The largest concentrations of shops are in Valletta, Sliema and Rabat.

## Valletta

### Open-air Markets

There are two open air markets in Valletta. Triq il-Merkanti (Merchants Street) is mostly clothes and accessories, religious icons, CDs and videos and there is little else of consumer interest. On Sunday a very busy market opens up in St James' Ditch, near the Triton Fountain, and although it does get frenzied at times there is also a more interesting collection of bric-à-brac, which might appeal to visitors, who will also enjoy watching the activity.

✉ **Triq il-Merkanti (Merchants Street) and St James' Ditch, Valletta**

🕐 **Triq il-Merkanti: Mon–Sat 7–noon; St James' Ditch: Sun 6:30–1PM**

### Indoor Market

Valletta's indoor market is mostly devoted to food and this is the place to visit the day before you leave Malta to make a last-minute purchase of *gbejna* (Gozitan cheese). It may not be available in sealed packets but it will keep fresh for the flight home and once put in the refrigerator the shelf life of this cheese is at least one month. The peppered version (*tal-bzar*) is recommended for those who prefer a much stronger cheese.

✉ **Triq il-Merkanti (Merchants Street) where the open air market ends**

🕐 **Mon–Sat 6:30–PM**

## Around Malta

### Marsaxlokk Open Air Market

Basically a fish market, but worth a visit even for those who are not actually making a purchase. The variety of shapes and colours of the Mediterranean fish here is surprising, making an attractive scene; and what you see here may well end up on your own plate when you visit one of Marsaxlokk's excellent fish restaurants.

✉ **Along the water front, Marsaxlokk**

🕐 **Sun 7–11:30AM**

🚌 **27 from Valletta, 427 from Buġibba, 627 from Paceville**

### Other Open-air Markets

Many towns in Malta have an open air market once or twice a week and they are worth visiting if you are in the area, but do not go out of your way to make a special trip. They are not tourist markets, but they do provide a welcome opportunity to mix with Maltese people going about the daily business of shopping and meeting friends.

✉ **Birkirkara, near the Church of St Helen**

🕐 **Wed, Fri 7–11AM**

🚌 **41, 42, 71, 78**

✉ **Birżebbuġa, in St Catherine Street near the Government Primary School**

🕐 **Thu 7–11AM**

🚌 **11, 115**

✉ **Naxxar, 21st September Ave**

🕐 **Thu 7–11AM**

🚌 **54, 55, 56, 65**

✉ **Rabat, opposite St Paul's Parish Church**

🕐 **Sat 7–11AM**

🚌 **80, 81, 83, 84, 86, 65**

✉ **Vittoriosa, St Margherita Heights**

🕐 **Tue 7–11AM**

🚌 **1, 2, 4, 6**

# Handicrafts, Arts & Antiques

## Valletta

### Artisans Centre

A few doors away from the tourist information office is one of the best shops for a general selection of handicrafts. The jewellery section has handsome Maltese crosses on chains. Picture frames, prints, souvenirs and gifts are also available.

✉ **9 and 10 Freedom Square and 288 Republic Street, Valletta** ☎ **21246216** ⊙ **Mon–Fri 9–1, 4–7, Sat 9–1**

### Galea Paintings

The studio and gallery of the artist Aldo Galea. The subject is Malta, especially shipping scenes. The work sells for between LM15 and LM150. A posting and packing service can also be arranged.

✉ **8 Merchants Street, Valletta** ☎ **21243591** ⊙ **Mon–Fri 9:30–1, 4–7, Sat 9:15–12:45**

### Gio. Batta Delia

Fine chinaware and glass from around the world – Wedgwood, Waterford, Spode, Belleek, Minton, Dresden, Cristal Lalique – and an export service. There is also a small branch in Sliema at 76 Tigne Street (☎ 21332924).

✉ **Ferreria Palace, 307 Republic Street, Valletta** ☎ **21233618**

### The Silversmith's Shop

One of the few remaining Maltese jewellers making items such as chains and earrings by hand in traditional styles.

✉ **218 Republic Street, Valletta** ☎ **21231416** ⊙ **Mon–Fri 10–7, Sat–Sun 10–3**

## Around Malta

### Empire Arts and Crafts Centre

This huge crafts emporium sells just about everything. The lace work, paintings, glass and ceramics take second place to the largest selection of jewellery in Malta. Necklaces, brooches, earrings, bangles and talismans are here, plus an astounding variety of watches. Craftspeople make lace, glass and silver filigree. Highly recommended.

✉ **20A/B St Agatha Street, Rabat** ☎ **21453245** ⊙ **Mon–Sat 10–6** 🚌 **80, 81, 83, 84, 86**

### Galleria Cremona

Marco Cremona is a Maltese artist, born in 1951, who studied in Italy and London and worked as an art teacher before turning professional. His paintings have been exhibited in Europe and his work, usually impressions of Malta, sells for between LM75 and LM500; prints are a lot less expensive.

✉ **16 Museum Road, Rabat** ☎ **21451280** ⊙ **Summer: Mon–Sat 10–6** 🚌 **80, 81, 83, 84, 86**

### Greenhand Leathercraft

This little shop, bound to be passed on a walk through Mdina (► 60), has two branches inside the city walls. The action in the workshop can be seen and, as well as leather goods, some lace and gifts are also on sale.

✉ **2 Magazine Street and 28 Villegaigon Street, Mdina** ☎ **21454689** ⊙ **Mon–Sat 10–6**

## What to Buy

Maltese handicrafts are the best items to take home. Apart from the glass, choose from filigree silver jewellery, Maltese crosses, gold jewellery, lace work and ceramics. Italian clothes tend to predominate in the boutiques in Sliema.

## Glass

One of the best buys is glass and there are three main types. The blue and green Mdina glass is probably the most widely distributed in shops and it can be seen being made at Ta' Qali (► right). Phoenician glass, a characteristic deep blue, is made on Manoel Island (► 50) and is also available in good shops. Vibrantly coloured Gozo glass, the most expensive, is best purchased on Gozo (► right).

### Lin's Lace

Some of the small craft shops in Mdina keep irregular hours but Lin's Lace can be relied upon throughout the year for jewellery, crafts, local wine, pottery and garments. You'll find the shop in the lane that leads from near the cathedral to the Craft Centre.

🖂 Triq Bieb, Mdina ☎ 21563022 🕐 Mon–Sat 9:30–5

### Mdina Glass

Decorative glass is made here in the traditional manner by hand and mouth; also etching and crystal cutting.

🖂 Ta' Qali Craft Village, Ta' Qali
☎ 21415786 🕐 Jun–Oct, Mon–Fri 8–6, Sat 8–12:30, Sun 9–4 (Mar–Oct); Nov–Jun, Mon–Fri 8–4, Sat 8–12:30
🚌 80 from Valletta or Rabat; 86 from Bugibba; 65 from Sliema

### Phoenician Glassblowers

Even if no purchase is made, it is still interesting to watch the fascinating process of glass being mouth-blown and handmade. The beautiful blues and yellows of the glass are many visitors' favourites.

🖂 Ta' Qali Crafts Village, Hut 10 ☎ 21437041 🕐 Mon–Sat 9–4:30

### Ta' Qali Craft Village

The site is a disused airfield from World War II and the crews' Nissen huts are now devoted to the peaceful business of retailing lace, glass and other crafts. Mdina Glass have their workshop here.

🖂 Ta' Qali ☎ 22141111
🕐 Mon–Fri 8–4:30, Sat 8–12:30

## Gozo

### Bastion Lace

More than one little shop sells handicrafts in the Citadel, but only attractive hand-made lace is sold in this delightfully tiny shop. Friendly service, no undue pressure to buy.

🖂 Bieb l-Imdina Street, Citadel, Gozo
☎ 21561471
🕐 Mon–Sat 9:30–5

### The Fort Lai Thai

Come to Gozo and leave with handicrafts from Thailand or India! Lots of items small enough to fit into your luggage and an adjoining snack bar to pause and consider before making a final decision.

🖂 G. Borg Street, Victoria, Gozo ☎ 21553313
🕐 Mon–Sat 9–4:30

### Gozo Glass

The glass-making workshop is on show inside the shop. Some people find Gozo glass gaudy and flashy, but there are beautiful examples to be found here, and a visit is recommended. The shop is on the main road just outside Gharb on the road to Victoria.

🖂 Triq Il-Gharb, Gozo ☎ 21561974 🕐 Mon–Sat 9–6 (Workshop closes at 3:30, Sun 10–4) 🚌 2, 91

### Joe Xuereb

Hand-carved and hand-decorated sculptures using Gozo stone. The best pieces look as if they might be thousands of years old, and not cheap. Situated in the village of Għajnsielem, reached by turning right into Għajnsielem Street from the main road to Victoria shortly after leaving the ferry at Mġarr.

🖂 Ta' Peppi, Bahhara Street, Għajnsielem, Gozo ☎ 21553559
🕐 Daily 10–4

### Ta' Dbiegi Craft Village

Heading west from Victoria, take the left fork after passing the turn-off for Ta' Pinu Church. The craft village is on the left of the main road before reaching San Lawrenz. There is nothing craft-like about the premises: characterless low-level British military huts converted into shops. Pottery, art, lace and clothes account for most of the merchandise.

✉ **On the main road between Ta'Pinu Church and San Lawrenz** ☎ 21556202
🕐 Daily 8:30–6:45
🚌 2, 91 from Victoria

## Souvenirs & Shopping Centres

### Valletta
**Gopaldas Oriental Bazaar**
Two floors of gifts from Malta and the Orient. There is little of real quality but for inexpensive souvenirs and gifts the place is worth a quick browse.

✉ **33 Republic Street, Valletta** ☎ 21224938
🕐 Mon–Sat 9:30–7, Sun (Apr–Oct) 10–1

## Around Malta
**Aladdin's Cave**
There are souvenirs galore plus gifts in this popular, inexpensive tourist shop. There are also knitted woollen garments for sale for those who can overcome the psychological barrier of contemplating them when the island's temperatures are ferocious.

✉ **79 Triq Ir-Rebbiengha, Buġibba** ☎ 21573617
🕐 Mon–Sat 10–9 (winter 10–7); Sun 10–4 (summer only) 🚌 49 from Valletta, 48 from Ċirkewwa, 51 from Għajn Tuffieħa, 70, 645, 652, from Sliema, 86 between Buġibba and Rabat, 427 between Buġibba and Marsaxlokk

**Baystreet Shopping Centre**
With a hotel, several eateries, IMAX cinema and a smattering of up-market names, this is Malta's classiest shopping mall and is very popular with locals and tourists. There's an artisan market on the ground floor selling traditional crafts and souvenirs.

✉ **Bay Street, St George's Bay, St Julian's** ☎ 21380600
🕐 Mon–Sat 9–9 (entertainment longer hours)

**J M Jewellers**
You'll find a reasonable range of affordable jewellery in this well-positioned shop on the promenade. There is another jewellers a few doors down, so prices can be compared.

✉ **30 Islets Promenade, Buġibba** ☎ 21583863
🕐 Jun–Sep, Mon–Sun 9–10; closing earlier during the winter.

**Plaza Shopping Centre**
Currently Malta's largest shopping centre has a range of well-known fashion names, plus smaller family-owned stores. Worth a browse for shopaholics.

✉ **Bisazza Street, Sliema** ☎ 21343832 🕐 Mon–Sat 9–7

## Gozo
**Arkadia Shopping Centre**
This is the largest shopping centre on Gozo and here you will find a department store, boutiques, shoewear shops and a fast-food outlet. There is a smaller shopping centre in the complex that is home to the Gozo tourist office (▶ 120).

✉ **Fortunato Mizzi (end of Republic Street)**
☎ 22103000 🕐 Mon–Sat 9–7

### Lace
Gozo is renowned for its hand-made lace, a traditional home-based activity that began life as a devotional act by pious women making lace adornments for their local church. Shawls and tablecloths are the most popular items and prices are reasonable. Rabat in Malta and the Citadel in Gozo are the best places to make a purchase.

# Dolphins, Dungeons, Leisure Parks & Rides

### Multi-Media Events
Older children should enjoy some of the multi-media 'experiences' (▶ 110). They manage to be educational as well as entertaining, and the souvenir shop at the Malta Experience could empty purses of pocket money. The Wartime Experience (▶ 110) is best reserved for teenagers.

### Beaches
The Mediterranean has virtually no tide and the beaches are generally safe for children. The sandy beaches are: Armier Bay, Mellieha Bay, Golden Bay (all with lifeguards in summer), Paradise Bay, Għajn Tuffieħa Bay and Gnejne Bay, all in the northern part of the island; Pretty Bay (lifeguard) and St Thomas Bay in the south; Ramla Bay on Gozo. Paddleboats, safe for older children, can be hired at Armier Bay, Mellieha Bay, Golden Bay and Għajn Tuffieħa Bay.

### Club Neptune
A waterpolo and swimming club open to non-members on a daily membership basis. The fresh-water pool is heated and there are restaurant and bar facilities. It is located near the Barracuda restaurant on the waterfront, and parents might wish to retire across the road to the City of London café and bar while their children frolic.
✉ Balluta Bay, St Julian's
☎ 21346900 ◷ Daily 8–5
🚌 62, 64, 67, 68, 70 from Valletta, 627 between Paceville and Marsaxlokk

### Eden Super Bowl and Cinemas
Consisting of a computerised bowling alley with 20 lanes, a bar and a huge multi-cinema complex (that even spreads to the other side of the road), Eden makes an evening's entertainment for the young. The Paceville location means plenty of fast-food type restaurants close by.
✉ Paceville, St George's Bay
☎ 21387398 ◷ Daily 10AM–12:30AM 🚌 62, 64, 67, 68, 70

from Valletta, 627 between Paceville and Marsaxlokk

### Fort Rinella
Volunteers in 19th-century costume conduct a tour of the fort and conclude with a bayonet practise display with non-obligatory audience participation. Visitors can use the weapons (LM1 per round) but not at each other!
www.wirtartna.org
✉ St Rocco Road, Kalkara ☎ 21809713; ◷ Mon–Sat 10–4; tours at 11:10 and 2:30; activity tour Tue and Sat 2:30 🚌 4 from Valletta and a 10-minute walk

### Helicopter Ride
One possibility is to combine transport with pleasure and take the children to and from Gozo via helicopter, departing from Malta's international airport and arriving at the Xewkija heliport in Gozo. The fare for children under 12 is 50 per cent of the adult fare. A discount is given for students with a student card. Sightseeing helicopter flights lasting either 20 or 40 minutes are also available.
✉ Malta Air Charter, Luqa ☎ 21662211 (Air Malta), 21557905 (Gozo Heliport), 21243777 (Valletta), 21330646 (Sliema) ◷ Daily

### Karting
For older children, karting is a thrilling sport, made all the more exciting if they can beat Mum or Dad in competition. Karts can be rented for 15 minutes or longer, and all safety equipment is provided.
✉ Badger Karting, Duramblatt Street, Mosta (track at Ta'Qali Centre) ☎ 21421838; www.badger.com.mt
✉ Team Adventures,

**1113 St Joseph's Street, Pieta**
☎ 21248725
✉ **Island Karting Club, 124 Old Theatre Street, Valletta**
☎ 21544966

## Mdina Dungeons

Pass through Mdina Gate and these medieval dungeon chambers are immediately on one's right: 'Discover Horror, Drama and Mysteries from the dark past'. Young children will love the waxwork scenarios and their gruesome details.
✉ **St Publius Square, Mdina**
☎ 21450267 ◷ **Daily 9:30–5:30**
🚌 **80, 83, 86**

## Mediterranean Marine Park

Dolphins and sea lions, reptiles, swans, wallabies and other creatures are found cavorting here and putting on shows each day.
✉ **White Rocks, Bahar ic-Caghaq** ☎ 21372218
◷ **Apr–Oct, 10–5; check in winter** 🚌 **70 from Sliema or Buġibba, 68 from Valletta**

## Playmobil FunPark

The German lego-like toy company has a shop, play area and water channels to amuse young children. Tours of the toy factory are sometimes available but telephone ahead to check.
✉ **HS 80 Hol-Far Industrial Estate, Hol-Far** ☎ 22242387
◷ **Jul–Sep, Mon–Fri 9–6, Sat 6–9PM; Oct–Jun, Mon–Fri 9–5:30**
🚌 **27–30**

## Splash and Fun Park

Next door to the Mediterranean Marine Park, with four water chutes, large pool, restaurant. Adjacent, the Children's Play park is free to enter: model dinosaurs, bouncy castles, bumper cars and the like.
✉ **White Rocks, Bahar ic-Caghaq** ☎ 21374283 ◷ **Daily 10–7** 🚌 **70 from Sliema or Buġibba, 68 from Valletta**

## Sun City

A leisure centre in Marsaskala comprising four cinemas, a snooker table and a café serving snacks.
✉ **Triq Il-Gardiel, Marsaskala**
☎ 21632858
◷ **Daily 10–2, 6:30–11 (later closing summer weekends)**
🚌 **19, 20, 22**

## Toy Museum

There is little in Gozo that is specifically aimed at children but that is not a reason for thinking of not visiting the island with young ones. The journey there, by boat or helicopter (▶ 108), is pleasantly short and interesting and once on Gozo the Citadel at Victoria has plenty of museums (▶ 84) suitable for children. There is a Toy Museum in Xagħra for younger children (▶ 89). The Gozo 360° audio-visual show on the history and culture of Gozo (▶ 111) is another possibility.
✉ **Xagħra, Gozo** ☎ 21562489
◷ **Apr–May, Thu–Sat 10–1; Jun–Oct, Mon–Sat 10–12, 3–6; Nov–Mar, Mon–Sat 10–1** 🚌 **64, 65 from Victoria**

## Underwater Safari

Children should enjoy a trip in MV *Seabelow's* observation keel, for it is below the level of the sea with windows for viewing the marine life, including the odd passing octopus. The boat has a feeding system that keeps fish in its vicinity so there is always something to see amid the algae. Every passenger has at least 20 minutes in the observation keel during the one-hour trip.
✉ **Captain Morgan Cruises, Dolphin Court, Tigne Seafront, Sliema** ☎ 21343373
◷ **Departure from Buġibba from 10AM onwards** 🚌 **Sliema: 60–64, 67, 68 from Valletta, 70, 86 from Buġibba, 65, 86 from Rabat, 645 from Ċirkewwa, 652 from Golden Bay, Buġibba**

## Discotheques

The usual pattern for Malta's discos is to allow people in for free before about 10PM and until at least 11PM there are few people over 21 on the dance floor. This makes them ideal for teenagers who can safely enjoy the sound and lighting effects and the videos (▶ 113 for details of the more popular discos).

# Trips & Shows, Casinos & Cruises

**A Day Trip to Sicily?**
Day trips to Sicily, using a catamaran to make the crossing in 1.5 hours, depart early in the morning and arrive back in Malta late at night. The trip usually includes various excursions by coach to places like Mount Etna. Some visitors have found it an exhausting day and an expensive one.

## Valletta

### The Malta Experience

If time and inclination restrict you to visiting just one of the multilingual audio-visual, large-screen presentations about Malta and Gozo then this is the one to see. The theatre is set inside the historic 16th-century Sacra Infermeria (► 40) and the show sets itself the daunting task of presenting Malta's history from Neolithic times onwards in 50 minutes. With the help of 3, 000 colour slides and 39 projectors it does this well. There is access for visitors with disabilities and you will also find a restaurant and souvenir shop.

www.themaltaexperience.com
✉ St Elmo Bastion, Mediterranean Street, Valetta
☎ 21243776 ◷ Mon–Fri on the hour 11–4, Sat-Sun 11–1PM. Also Sun 2PM Oct–Jan

### St James Cavalier Centre for Creativity

Films, theatre, music recitals and art exhibitions take place on a regular basis during the day and there are evening events. There is a shop and a coffee bar, not open at weekends.
✉ Ordnance Street ☎ 21223200; info@sjcav.org
◷ Mon–Sat 10–10, Sun 10–5

### The Wartime Experience

A film covering Malta during the years of World War II and made up of archive film recording what happened the and suffering endured by the Maltese people. Highly recommended.
✉ Embassy Complex, St Lucia's Street, Valletta ☎ 21227436 ◷ Mon–Sat 10–noon

## Around Malta

### Casinos

The Dragonara Casino, Malta's original casino, has a bar and restaurant and a dress code that stipulates that a jacket and tie must be worn (these can be borrowed if necessary). The Oracle casino is more geared towards tourists. There are a number of bars and restaurants, and the dress code here is smart/casual, with no shorts after 8PM.

www.dragonara.com
✉ Dragonara Casino, St Julian's ☎ 21382362
◷ 8:30–4AM
🚌 62, 64, 67, 68, 70 from Valletta, 627 between Paceville and Marsaxlokk. Free transport from Sliema and St Julian's
www.oraclecasino.com
✉ Oracle Casino, Qawra Seafront, St Paul's Bay
☎ 21570057
◷ Sun–Thu 10:AM–4PM, Fri-Sat 10AM–6AM

### Club de Bingo

Bingo halls do not come any posher than this one, which is easy to find as it is situated opposite the Dolmen hotel in Qawra.
✉ Dolmen Street, Qawra Seafront, Qawra ☎ 21577677
◷ Daily 10–11

### Cruises

Captain Morgan is a well-established tour company offering a variety of cruises on a regular basis. Harbour cruises depart from Sliema daily, from 10:30AM, and there is also a daily day-long cruise around Malta and the island of Comino, a Blue Lagoon cruise, sunset cruise, overnight cruise, a Party Boat

that departs Sliema at 8:30PM and an underwater safari (▶ 109). Harbour cruises and other trips are also run by Luzzo Cruises from Marsaskala.

www.captainmorgan.com.mt

✉ Captain Morgan Cruises, Dolphin Court, Tigne Seafront, Sliema ☎ 21343373;

🚌 60, 61, 62, 63, 64, 67, 68 from Valletta, 70 from Buġibba, 65 from Rabat, 86 from Buġibba and Rabat, 645 from Ċirkewwa, 652 from Golden Bay

⛴ Valletta-Sliema ferry (☎ 23463333)

✉ Luzzo Cruises, 29 Marina Promenade, Marsaskala ☎ 21632669

### Discovery Package

This is the place to come for an action packed day out, including both a Jeep Safari with a tour leader and Captain Morgan's Underwater Safari (▶ 109). The price includes a typical Maltese lunch and transport to and from your accommodation. Departures are at approximately 9:30AM from the Jeep Safari terminal. During the summer trips take place Monday to Friday, check when operating at other times of the year.

Details as for Captain Morgan Cruises, above.

### The Mdina Experience

An audiovisual, multilingual spectacular spanning some 3,000 years of Mdina's history in half an hour. This is presented in a suitably ancient building. The presentation covers the Roman and Arab periods of occupation, the Knights of Malta, French and British rule. There is a coffee shop and a gift shop with an array of souvenirs. The 30-minute programme runs continuously every half an hour during the opening times.

www.themdinaexperience.com

✉ 7 Mesquita Square, Mdina ☎ 21454322 ⓖ Mon–Fri

10:30–4, Sat 10:30–3

🚌 80, 83, 86 from Valletta, 65 from Sliema

## Gozo

### Boat Trips

Pleasure trips lasting half a day or a full day depart from Mġarr harbour and cover Gozo, the island of Comino and the Blue Lagoon. Fishing trips and watersports are also available. There are meeting points for free transport at Xlendi and Marsalforn at 9:45AM.

www.xlendicruises.com

✉ Xlendi Pleasure Cruises ☎ 21559967;

ⓖ Dep 11, return 5:30

🚌 21 from Victoria for Marsalforn; 87 for Xlendi

### Gozo 360° – Island of Joy

Not to be outdone by similar shows in Valletta and Mdina, Gozo now has its very own sound-and-vision show designed to bring the smaller island's own culture and history to life. The presentation lasts just under half an hour with a multi-lingual commentary.

✉ Castle Hill, Rabat, Gozo ☎ 21559955

ⓖ Mon–Sat, every hour between 10:30 and 4:30, Sun every hour between 10:30 and 1:30 🚌 25 from Mġarr

### Sunset Cruise

The boat leaves Mġarr, in July and August, in the evening and the first port of call is the island of Comino. Gozo cheese and hobz biz-zejt (bread with oil, pulped tomato, olives and seasonings) are one way to keep hunger pangs at bay as the boat proceeds along the coast, and then to Comino where it anchors for dinner.

✉ Frankie's Gozo Diving Centre ☎ 21551315

ⓖ Dep 5PM, return 11PM

🚌 25 from Victoria

### Hollywood of the Mediterranean

Malta has become the location for a number of Hollywood blockbusters, including Gladiator (2000), starring Russell Crowe, and Troy (2004), starring Brad Pitt, as well as BBC dramas like Daniel Deronda and Byron. Full details of the various locations can be accessed via www.visitmalta.com.

# Bars & Discos

### Bars and Pubs
The British influence means that pubs are not uncommon in Malta or Gozo and there is tremendous variety in the kind of entertainment they offer. The smallest village is likely to have a tiny bar where visitors are welcome but the only diversion will be a conversation with fellow customers. Valletta's nightlife is non-existent, so for bright lights and live music head for Paceville (pronounced *PATCH-eh-vill*) or Buġibba.

## Bars

### Malta
#### Bar Native
This pub in Paceville does not encourage the under-25s and the music is not so loud that you cannot hear yourself speak. Wine by the glass or bottle and six types of draught beer. Sofas, bar stools and outdoor tables.
🔲 St George's Road, Snata Rita Steps, Paceville ☎ 21380635
◎ Daily 11–late (winter 6:30–late)

#### Baywatch Bar and Restaurant
An atmospheric place overlooking the quayside of Marsaxlokk, with a restaurant attached.
🔲 5–6 Xatt is-Sajjieda, Marsaxlokk ☎ 21653770
◎ Daily 11–11

#### B.J.s
This pub has a soul. There is a small stage for bands, often very good, and usually a pleasant upbeat atmosphere despite the dark and smoky interior. Jazz evenings featured. Recommended.
🔲 Ball Street, Paceville, St Julian's ☎ 21337642
◎ Daily, 7–late 🚌 62, 64, 67, 68, 70 from Valletta, 627 between Paceville and Marsaxlokk

#### The Pub
Also known as Ollie's Last Stand, as this was the pub where actor Oliver Reed collapsed and died during the filming of the Hollywood blockbuster *Gladiator*. Photos of the star adorn the walls of this tiny pub.
🔲 136 Archbishop Street, Valletta

☎ 21237525
◎ Daily 10–4

#### Saddles Pub
This pub has been around for a long time and, as one of the photographs on the wall makes clear, was once very popular with the British army. Still lively with a good atmosphere.
🔲 G. Borg Oliver Street, St Julian's ☎ 21339993
◎ Daily, 9–3AM 🚌 62, 64, 67, 68, 70 from Valletta, 627 between Paceville and Marsaxlokk

### Gozo
#### Il-Kartell
One of the more popular little bars in Marsalforn and a lively enough place as the night wears on. There is a billiards table and, although there is only taped music, sitting on the balcony and sipping drinks in this picturesque fishing village is a pleasant way to spend an evening.
🔲 Marsalforn waterfront ☎ 21556918 ◎ 8:30PM–1AM
🚌 21 from Victoria

#### The Rook
Set in an old fort by the sea, The Rook is one of Gozo's better nightclubs. Also worth a look in this area is Cocktails and Dreams on the Marsalforn seafront.
🔲 Qbajjar, Marsalforn ☎ 21563769 ◎ Mon–Sun 7–Late

### Buġibba-Qawra
While the Paceville area is popular with hip young Maltese, the Buġibba-Qawra area attracts mostly tourists. Hotels like the Suncrest and the Coastline (► 101, 102) provide floor shows. There is also dancing and live music from country and western to karaoke.

WHERE TO BE ENTERTAINED

▨ **Coastline, Salina Bay, Salina** ☎ 21573781

### Double Deuce Café
This is a bustling sports bar, with live big-screen football and regular karaoke evenings. A wide range of beers is on offer to a lively holiday crowd.

▨ **Carolina Hotel, St Anthony Street (dedicated bar entrance on Winter Street), Buġibba**
☎ 21571534
Ⓞ **Daily 11AM–late**

## Discos

### Malta
#### The Amazonia Club
The Dolmen Resort Hotel hosts one of the most popular late-night dancing scenes, with music from house to hip-hop to salsa.

▨ **Dolmen Resort Hotel, Qawra** ☎ 23552355 Ⓞ **Daily 8–late, summer only** 🚌 **48, 49, 51, 70**

#### Axis
Apart from the main dance floor, there is also the Freestyle club that plays less frantic music and, up on the floor above, a small designer-style bar with a tiny dance space and Salsa music setting the mood. Open every night through the summer, Axis has been around a long time and has regained its popularity.

▨ **Triq San Gorg, St Julian's**
Ⓞ **9:30–4AM** ☎ 21318078
🚌 **62, 64, 67, 68, 70 from Valletta, 627 between Paceville & Marsaxlokk**

#### Fuego Salsa Bar
This early evening shot bar turns into one of the hottest late-night venues with more than a touch of Latin feel.

▨ **Bajja San Gorg, St Julian's**
☎ 21386746 Ⓞ **Wed–Sat 6–late**

### Havana
One of the hottest new venues in this ever-changing young scene, Havana offers a great bar and a range of the latest sounds.

▨ **Triq San Gorg, Paceville**
☎ 21375450 Ⓞ **Wed–Sat 10–late**

### NaaSHa
An excellent venue or 'event lounge' with a range of sounds and live perform-ances, incorporating music genres from rock to jazz to reggae, and also live stand-up. Check out the weekly programme on their website.
www.naasha.com

▨ **Misrah Lourdes, San Gwann**
☎ 21373859 Ⓞ **Wed–Sun 9–late**

### Reeds
This popular open-air disco in Marsaskala is on the road to St Thomas Bay.

▨ **Triq Il-Gardiel, Marsaskala**
☎ 21684482 Ⓞ **Fri–Sun 8–late**
🚌 **19, 20, 22, 87**

## Gozo
### La Grotta
Not the most advanced sound system, but this open-air disco is delightful. An amazing location, with the bar in a cave, and a separate pub two minutes away. Opens at 11PM but doesn't come alive until early the next morning.

▨ **Xlendi Road, Xlendi, Gozo**
☎ 21551149 Ⓞ **11PM–6:30AM**
🚌 **87 from Victoria**

### Buġibba Bars
The place to be for young folk in Buġibba is where Pioneer Road meets the promenade. A cluster of popular bars and numerous eating places near by makes this a natural meeting place and drinkers from pubs like the Bonkers, Coconut Creek and the Victoria spill outside and loudly share the pavement.

# Sports

## Health Clubs

A number of the better hotels have health and leisure clubs and some of them can boast excellent facilities. The best of all is the Myo Ka Spa at the Corinthia Hotel St Julian's (▶ 100) but the following are also very good: Livingwell Fitness Centre at the Hilton Hotel; the World Class Fitness Centre and Thalassoterapie Spa at the Fortina Hotel (☎ 21343380); the Kempinski San Lawrenze Hotel in Gozo (☎ 22110000; www.kempinski-gozo.com). Some of these operate a temporary membership scheme.

## Athletics

### The Malta Amateur Athletics Association

It is worth contacting the association to see what events are being organised during your stay. Cross-country and track-and-field events are held regularly.
**www.athleticsmalta.org**
✉ **7 Racecourse Street, Marsa** ☎ **22125214** 🚍 **43, 44, 45, 49, 53, 56, 57**

## Bowling

For a game of 10-pin bowling visit the Eden Super Bowl (▶ 108). There is a shop selling equipment, and a licensed bar.

## Cycling

There are no designated cycling lanes or bicycle trails, but Gozo is especially appealing and bikes can be hired from:

**Curtis Rent-a-Car**
✉ **94 Old College Street, St Julian's** ☎ **21331253**

**Freewheels Bike Centre**
✉ **Valletta Road, Mosta** ☎ **21416801**

**Hollywood Rent a Car/Jeep/Bike**
✉ **95 Sliema Ferry, Sliema** ☎ **21318704**

## Diving

Scuba divers are well catered for and 30- and 40-metre dives can be enjoyed with clear visibility. A useful brochure from the tourist board has a map showing the most popular dive sites and other helpful information.

### Professional Diving School Association

Has details of all registered diving companies.
**www.dig.gate.net/divers**
✉ **Msida Court, 61–2 Msida Sea Front, Msida** ☎ **21336441**

### Dive Clubs/Schools

There are many CMAS- or PADI- certified schools in Malta and Gozo. Some well-established diving clubs include:
**Dive Med**
**www.divemed.com** ✉
**Marsascala, Malta** ☎ **21639981**

### Strand Diving Services

**www.scubamalta.com**
✉ **St Paul's Bay, Malta** ☎ **21574502**

### Meldives

**Mellieha**
**www.digigate.net/meldives**
☎ **21522595**

### St Andrews Divers

**www.gozodive.com** ✉ **Xlendi Bay, Gozo** ☎ **21551301**

### Atlantis Diving Centre

**www.atlantisgozo.com**
✉ **Marsalforn, Gozo**
☎ **21554685**

## Golf

Golf was introduced to Malta by the Governor in 1888 and a nine-hole course was established in Floriana. The present 18-hole course at the Marsa Sports Club was re-grassed a few years ago and some 50 sand bunkers were added. Temporary membership at the Marsa Sports Club (▶ 115) allows visitors to use the course and there is a useful brochure from the tourist board that describes the nine most interesting holes.

### Royal Malta Golf Club

✉ **Marsa Sports Club, Aldo Moro St, Marsa** ☎ **21227019**

🚌 **1, 2, 3, 4, 5, 6, 8, 11, 12, 13, 15, 18, 19, 21, 26, 29, 32, 34, 35, 36**

## Sports Centres

### Marsa Sports Club

The island's largest sports centre, 4km south of Valletta, with Malta's only 18-hole golf course, cricket ground, mini golf, 18 tennis courts, 5 squash courts, billiards, fitness centre and a swimming pool. There is also a bar and restaurant. Visitors may join on a daily/weekly basis. Golf tuition is available.

**www.marsasportsclub.com**

✉ **Aldo Moro Street, Marsa** ☎ **21233851**

🕐 **Mon–Fri 9–9, Sat–Sun 9–5**

🚌 **1, 2, 3, 4, 5, 6, 8, 11, 12, 13, 15, 18, 19, 21, 26, 27, 29, 32, 34, 35, 36**

## Soccer

Soccer is very popular and games are mostly played between September and May. The National Stadium is the best place to view a match but games are also played elsewhere.

**Malta Football Association**

**www.mfa.com.mt**

✉ **280 St Paul Street, Valletta** ☎ **21222697;**

## Water Sports

### Sailing and Yachting

Between Malta, Gozo and Comino there are nearly 30 anchorages, and places to hire boats include Marsamxett Harbour and Mellieha Bay. Summer sailing regattas include the Comino regatta in June and the Malta-Syracuse race for keelboats in July. The Royal Malta Yacht Club at Manoel Island (☎ 21333109; www.rawsilk.com/rmyc) has information on the chartering of yachts. Enquire also at the Vikings Sailing Club Nautical

School, Floriana

☎ 21495003, Nautica

✉ 21–23 Msida Road, Gżira ☎ 21343821 or Malta Yacht Charter ☎ 21335771; www.maltayatchcharter.com

### Malta Sailing Club

✉ **Triq Spinola, St Julian's** ☎ **21382995**

### Sport Fishing

Fishing Mania has a boat insured for up to six people with a qualified captain. Leaves Marsaskala or Ta Xbiex at 8:30AM and arrives back in the afternoon.There is an 8:30PM departure for night bottom fishing, returning at 2AM. Rates include tackle, bait and snacks.

**www.mol.net.mt/Fishingmania**

✉ **Fishing Mania, 20, Flat 4, Old Anchor Court, Buttar Street, Marsaskala** ☎ **21632595** 🚌 **19, 20, 21**

### Water Skiing

Water skiing can be arranged through the larger hotels at St Paul's Bay, Mellieha Bay, Sliema, St George's Bay and Golden Bay. Between April and October, Paradise offer a range of watersports including water skiing, canoeing, windsurfing, pedal boating and snorkelling.

✉ **Paradise Diving and Watersports, Paradise Bay Hotel, Cirkewwa** ☎ **21574116; paradise@global.net.mt**

### Windsurfing

Windsurfing may be enjoyed at a number of hotels fronting the sheltered northern bays. The Ramia Bay Complex (☎ 21522181) has excellent facilities for water sports, including windsurfing. Others include St George's Park (☎ 21351147) and St Patrick's, Jerma (☎ 21562951). The watersports club at the Comino Hotel (☎ 21529822) gives lessons.

### Snorkelling and Diving

Both snorkellers and divers should fly a code-A flag or tow a surface marker buoy to alert speedboat traffic. Popular snorkelling spots include the west coast just north of Bahar-ic-Caghaq, while a more deserted place is the Għar Qawqla beach near the Hotel Calypso at Marsalforn, Gozo. Go past the hotel and up the flight of steps near the public toilets.

# What's On When

### Festas

Various aspects of a traditional *festa* will appeal to children, from the food stalls selling nougat to the colourful parades and the general carnival atmosphere. The firework displays – villagers try to out do each other – are especially dramatic and loud and not to be missed. Details of *festas* can be found listed in the *Malta Independent*.

### Victory Day

A commemorative ceremony is held in Valletta to celebrate the lifting of the 1565 siege against the Turks, the capitulation of the French in 1880 and the end of the siege of the Axis powers in 1943. A colourful and keenly contested boat race is held in Grand Harbour and *festas* are held in Sengla, Nexxar, Mellieha and Xaghra in Gozo.

## Public Holidays

Between May and October every town and village celebrates the feast day (*festa*) of its patron saint.

**1 Jan** New Year's Day

**10 Feb** Feast of Saint Paul's Shipwreck, Valletta

**31 Mar** Freedom Day

### Holy Week

Good Friday processions are held in various villages and towns around Malta and Gozo on the afternoon of Good Friday, a public holiday. Good Friday pageants are held in 14 different towns and villages featuring a number of life-sized statues depicting religious scenes. There will also be men and women in period costume personifying Biblical characters. Many places of entertainment are closed but cinemas and cafés remain open on Good Friday.

**1 May** Worker's Day

**29 Jun** Feast of St Peter and Paul. Parish *festa* in Nadur (Gozo)

**15 Aug** Feast of the Assumption. Parish *festas* in Attard, Ghaxaq, Gudja, Mgarr, Mosta, Mqabba, Qrendi, Victoria Cathedral (Gozo)

**8 Sep** Victory Day (► left)

**21 Sep** Independence Day

**8 Dec** Feast of the Immaculate Conception.

**13 Dec** Republic Day

**25 Dec** Christmas Day

## Other Parish *Festas* in Malta

☎ 21222644 for information and confirmation.

| | |
|---|---|
| **Balluta** | Last Sun in Jul |
| **Balzan** | 2nd Sun in Jul |
| **Birkirkara** | 1st Sun in Jul and 18 Aug |
| **Birżebbuġa** | 1st Sun in Aug |
| **Dingli** | 20 Aug |
| **Floriana** | 3rd Sun after Easter |
| **Għargħur** | 24th Aug or the Sun after |
| **Gzira** | 4 Jun |
| **Marsaskala** | 26 Jul or the Sun after |
| **Marsaxlokk** | 2nd Sun in Jul |
| **Mdina** | Last Sun in Jan |
| **Qormi** | Last Sun in Jun and 3rd Sun in Jul |
| **Rabat** | 1st Sun in Jul |
| **Sliema** | 2nd Fri of Lent, 1st and 3rd Sun in Jul, the Sun after 18 Aug and 1st Sun in Sep |
| **St Julian's** | Last Sun in Aug |
| **St Paul's Bay** | Last Sun in Jul |
| **Valletta** | 3rd Sun after Easter, 1st Sunday before 4 Aug |
| **Vittoriosa** | 10 Aug or the nearest Sun |
| **Żurrieq** | 1st Sun in Sep |

## Other Parish *Festas* in Gozo

| | |
|---|---|
| **Għarb** | 1st Sun in Jul |
| **San Lawrenz** | Last Sun in Jul |
| **Sannat** | 4th Sun in Jul |
| **Victoria** | 3rd Sun in Jul |
| **Xewkija** | 4th Sun in Jun |
| **Żebbuġ** | 20 Aug |

# Practical Matters

Above: *tile decoration, Mdina*
Right: *Xlendi statue*

117

## TIME DIFFERENCES

| GMT | Malta | Germany | USA (NY) | Netherlands | Spain |
|---|---|---|---|---|---|
| 12 noon | → 1PM | → 1PM | ← 7AM | → 1PM | → 1PM |

## BEFORE YOU GO

### WHAT YOU NEED

● Required
○ Suggested

Some countries require a passport to remain valid for a minimum period (usually at least six months) beyond the date of entry – contact their consulate or embassy or your travel agent for details.

| | UK | Germany | USA | Netherlands | Spain |
|---|---|---|---|---|---|
| Passport/National Identity Card | ● | ● | ● | ● | ● |
| Visa (regulations can change – check before making your trip) | ▲ | ▲ | ▲ | ▲ | ▲ |
| Onward or Return Ticket | ● | ● | ● | ● | ● |
| Health Inoculations | ▲ | ▲ | ▲ | ▲ | ▲ |
| Health Documentation (Reciprocal Agreement Document, ➤ 123, Health) | ▲ | ▲ | ▲ | ▲ | ▲ |
| Travel Insurance | ○ | ○ | ○ | ○ | ○ |
| Driving Licence (national or international) | ● | ● | ● | ● | ● |
| Car Insurance Certificate (if own car, specific to Malta) | ● | ● | ● | ● | ● |

### WHEN TO GO

**Malta**

High season

Low season

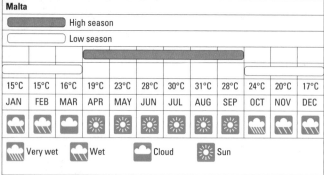

| 15°C | 15°C | 16°C | 19°C | 23°C | 28°C | 30°C | 31°C | 28°C | 24°C | 20°C | 17°C |
|---|---|---|---|---|---|---|---|---|---|---|---|
| JAN | FEB | MAR | APR | MAY | JUN | JUL | AUG | SEP | OCT | NOV | DEC |

Very wet    Wet    Cloud    Sun

### TOURIST OFFICES

**In the UK** (also responsible for Eire)
Malta Tourist Office,
Unit C Parkhouse,
14 Northfields,
London SW18 1DD
☎ 020 8877 6990
fax: 020 8874 9416
www.visitmalta.com
office.uk@visitmalta.com

**In the USA** (also Canada)
Malta National Tourist Office
300 Lanidex Plaza,
Parsippany
New Jersey 07054
☎ 973/884-0899
fax: 425/795-3425
www.visitmalta.com

**POLICE 112**

**FIRE 199 (in Gozo: 21562044)**

**AMBULANCE 196**

**AIR RESCUE: 21244371**     **SEA RESCUE: 21238797**

## WHEN YOU ARE THERE

### ARRIVING

The national airline, Air Malta (☎ 21690890), operates scheduled flights from major European cities; there are also charter flights. Gozo has no airport. There are ferry and catamaran services from southern Italy and Sicily to Malta (Valletta). Embarkation cards to be filled in *before* passport control.

| **Malta (Luqa) Airport** Kilometres to city centre | **Journey times** | |
|---|---|---|
| | 🚇 | N/A |
| **8 kilometres** | 🚌 | 20 minutes |
| | 🚕 | 15 minutes |

| **Grand Harbour (Valletta)** Kilometres to city centre | **Journey times** | |
|---|---|---|
| | 🚇 | N/A |
| **1 kilometre** | 🚌 | N/A |
| | 🚕 | 2 minutes |

### MONEY

The monetary unit of Malta is the Maltese lira (plural: liri), which is abbreviated to LM.
The lira is divided into 100 cents (c) and there is a further subdivision of cents into mils. Though there are no longer any mil coins you may come across them in prices. Coins are in denominations of 1, 2, 5, 10, 25 and 50 cents and 1 lira, and notes come in 2, 5, 10 and 20 liri. Malta plans to introduce the euro in 2008.

### TIME

Malta is one hour ahead of Greenwich Mean Time (GMT+1), but from late March, when clocks are put forward one hour, to late September, summer time (GMT +2) operates.

### CUSTOMS

**YES**
**From another EU country for personal use (guidelines)**
800 cigarettes, 200 cigars,
1 kilogram of tobacco
10 litres of spirits (over 22%)
20 litres of aperitifs
90 litres of wine, of which 60 litres can be sparkling wine
110 litres of beer

**From a non-EU country for your personal use, the allowances are:**
200 cigarettes OR
50 cigars OR 250 grams of tobacco
1 litre of spirits (over 22%)
2 litres of intermediary products (eg sherry) and sparkling wine
2 litres of still wine
50 grams of perfume
0.25 litres of eau de toilette

**Travellers under 17 years of age are not entitled to the tobacco and alcohol allowances.**

**NO**
Drugs, firearms, ammunition, offensive weapons, obscene material, unlicensed animals and certain foodstuffs.

## EMBASSIES/ HIGH COMMISSIONS

**UK**
23230000
(High Commission)

**Germany**
21336520 (Embassy)

**USA**
25614000
(Embassy)

**Spain**
39 06 6840401
(Resident in Rome)

## WHEN YOU ARE THERE

### TOURIST OFFICES

**Malta – Head Office**
● National Tourism
  Organisation
  Auberge d'Italie
  Merchants Street
  Valletta
  ☎ 22915000
  Fax: 22928393
  info@visitmalta.com
  www.visitmalta.com

**Local Tourist Information Offices**

**Malta**
● 1 City Arcades, Valletta
  ☎ 21237747

● Malta (Luqa) International
  Airport
  Arrivals Hall
  Gudja
  ☎ 23696073

**Gozo**
● Tigrija Palazz
  Republic Street
  Victoria (Rabat)
  ☎ 21561419

### NATIONAL HOLIDAYS

| J | F | M | A | M | J | J | A | S | O | N | D |
|---|---|---|---|---|---|---|---|---|---|---|---|
| 1 | 1 | (2/3) | (1) | 1 | 2 |  | 1 | 2 |  |  | 3 |

| | |
|---|---|
| 1 Jan | New Year's Day |
| 10 Feb | Feast of St Paul's Shipwreck |
| 19 Mar | Feast of St Joseph |
| 31 Mar | Freedom Day |
| Mar/Apr | Good Friday |
| 1 May | Workers' Day |
| 7 Jun | Sette Giugno (Commemoration of 7 June 1919) |
| 29 Jun | Feast of St Peter and St Paul |
| 15 Aug | Feast of the Assumption |
| 8 Sep | Victory Day |
| 21 Sep | Independence Day |
| 8 Dec | Feast of the Immaculate Conception |
| 13 Dec | Republic Day |
| 25 Dec | Christmas Day |

### OPENING HOURS

○ Shops    ● Restaurants
● Offices   ● Museums
● Banks    ● Cafés and Bars

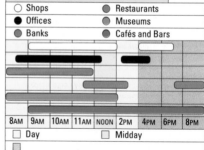

| 8AM | 9AM | 10AM | 11AM | NOON | 2PM | 4PM | 6PM | 8PM |
|---|---|---|---|---|---|---|---|---|

☐ Day        ☐ Midday

In addition to the times shown above, many shops in
tourist areas stay open throughout the day. In Valletta
shops close at 1PM Saturday, and except for a few in
Buġibba, shops are closed Sunday. Offices open
earlier but do not re-open for the afternoon during the
height of summer. Banks open 8:30AM to 12:45PM in
winter. Banks also open Friday 2:30 to 4PM (4:30 to
6PM, winter) and Saturday 8 to 11:30AM (8:30AM to
noon, winter). Banks, businesses, shops and
museums are closed on National Holidays.
Restaurants and bars remain open.

**DRIVE ON THE LEFT**

**TOILETS CHARGE**

## PUBLIC TRANSPORT

**Helicopter** The fastest and most convenient way to travel between Malta and Gozo is by helicopter (► 108).

**Trains** There are no train services available on Malta or Gozo.

**Cross-Island Buses** Most of Malta's towns and villages are connected to Valletta by bus. Fares are between 7c and 30c. Usually they depart from and return to City Gate (the main terminus). Buses (yellow with an orange stripe) are numbered but their destination is not shown. However, billboards showing the destination and route number can be found in the City Gate Bus Terminus and the tourist office dispenses a free bus map. On Gozo, buses (grey with a red stripe) serve the main villages from Victoria but only run in the morning. Bus passes for 1, 3, 5 and 7 days may be purchased at the Valletta or Bugibba terminals or the Sliema ferry terminal ☎ 21250007; www.atp.com.mt

**Ferries** Ferries from Malta to Gozo (Mġarr) depart from Ċirkewwa (20-minute crossing) or Sa Maison (75 minutes). Services are frequent. In summer there are also passenger-only hover-marine services from Sa Maison to Mġarr (25 minutes) and from Sliema (30 minutes); some trips via the island of Comino. For information of all services (☎ 21243964/5/6).

**Urban Transport** Valletta is the only major conurbation on Malta but as driving is virtually impossible around the city most people walk. From the main bus terminus at City Gate buses are destined for other parts of the island, except for bus 98, which follows a circular route around Valletta, and is probably your best bet.

## CAR RENTAL

Hire rates vary but as mileage and insurance is included, it is cheap for Europe. Companies such as Avis (☎ 21246640) and Europcar (☎ 21805350) accept credit cards. Signposting is poor and so is road quality.

## TAXIS

Mostly white Mercedes with distinctive 'taxi' sign on roof. They do not cruise but can be picked up at the airport, hotels, harbours, central ranks or by phone. Black taxis also operate, at cheaper rates, but need to be booked by telephone. Wembley Motors ☎ 21374141

## DRIVING

Speed limits: There are no motorways on Malta or Gozo.

Speed limits on country roads: **40mph (64kph)**

Speed limits in built-up areas: **24mph (40kph)**

Must be worn in front seats at all times and in rear seats where fitted.

Random breath-testing. Never drive under the influence of alcohol.

Petrol (super grade and unleaded) is readily available. Service stations open 7AM to 6PM (4PM Saturday); some to 7PM in summer. On Sundays and public holidays a few stations open on a rota basis 8AM to noon, so make sure you have enough fuel in the tank on Saturday night if planning an excursion. Petrol stations do not accept cheques or credit cards.

If you are involved in a road traffic accident, call the police immediately (☎ 112), and *do not* move the vehicle as it may invalidate your insurance. In the event of a breakdown there are two breakdown companies: RMF (☎ 21242222) and MTC (☎ 21320349). If you break down in a hired car, call the hire company to request help.

## PERSONAL SAFETY

You have little to fear in Malta since the crime rate is low and the Maltese are generally honest and courteous. The police (*pulizija*) – blue uniforms similar to British police – have a station in every town and village. Report any crime to them immediately. Some precautions:

- Leave valuables in the hotel or apartment safe, not on the beach.
- Don't make yourself an obvious target for bag-snatchers or pickpockets.
- Don't leave valuables visible in a car.

**Police assistance:**
☎ **191** (in Gozo: 56 20 44) from any call box

## TELEPHONES

Malta's public telephone boxes are either green, red or see-through booths. Few phones accept coins but most take a phonecard (*telecard*) available for LM2, LM3 or LM5 from Telemalta offices, post offices, banks and newsagents. All numbers in Malta and Gozo have 8 digits and there is no area code.

**International Dialling Codes**

| From Malta to: | |
| --- | --- |
| **UK**: | **00 44** |
| **Germany**: | **00 49** |
| **USA**: | **00 1** |
| **Netherlands**: | **00 31** |
| **Spain**: | **00 34** |

## POST

**Post Offices**
There are post offices in most towns and villages. The main post offices are in Merchants Street, Valletta (Malta) and 129 Republic Street, Victoria (Gozo), open later, otherwise hours are:
Open: 7:45–12:45
Closed: Sun
☎ Freephone 80072244

## ELECTRICITY

The local power supply is: 220/240 volts, 50Hz

Type of socket: 3-square-hole type taking square

plugs with 3 square pins (as used in the UK). Visitors from continental Europe should bring an adaptor; US visitors a voltage transformer.

## TIPS/GRATUITIES

| Yes ✓   No ✗ | | |
| --- | :---: | --- |
| Hotels (if service not included) | ✓ | (10%) |
| Restaurants (if service not included) | ✓ | (10%) |
| Cafés/bars | ✓ | (change) |
| Taxis | ✗ | |
| Porters | ✓ | (20c bag) |
| Chambermaids | ✓ | (50c wk) |
| Usherettes | ✗ | |
| Hairdressers | ✓ | (10%) |
| Cloakroom attendants | ✓ | (cents) |
| Toilets | ✓ | (cents) |

## PHOTOGRAPHY

**What to photograph:** The natural surroundings provide some dramatic settings – spectacular pastel-coloured cliffs contrasted by rich turquoise seas.

**Light:** The fierce light of the midday sun should be avoided; clear early morning light or the golden light of sunset are preferable.

**Film:** Film and digital peripherals are easily available, though slightly more expensive than in mainland Europe.

## HEALTH

### Insurance

Nationals of the UK and certain other countries staying less than 30 days receive free medical treatment within the Maltese health service, but prescribed medicines must be paid for. However, private medical insurance is advised for all.

### Dental Services

Dental treatment must be paid for. If you need a dentist enquire at the hotel reception desk or call directory enquiries (☎ 1182). Private medical insurance covers dental treatment and is advised for all visitors.

### Sun Advice

The Maltese Islands bask in virtual year-round sunshine; it is almost non-stop April to September. The sun is at its strongest during July and August when wearing a sunhat and covering up the skin is recommended. No topless/nude sunbathing is allowed.

### Drugs

In Malta, pharmacies, usually known as chemists, are recognisable by a neon green cross sign. They sell most international drugs and medicines over the counter or by prescription. They open normal shop hours with a Sunday roster.

### Safe Water

Tap water is quite safe though not very palatable. Water from fountains should be avoided as it may not come directly from the mains supply. Bottled 'table' water is available everywhere at a reasonable cost along with imported mineral water.

## CONCESSIONS

**Students/Youths** Holders of an International Student Identity Card (ISIC) can take advantage of concessions for students including reductions of between 15 and 40 per cent on transport, exhibitions, restaurants and shops, while entrance to museums is free.

**Senior Citizens** Malta, a popular destination for senior citizens, offers low-cost long-stay winter packages. However, apart from a reduction on some museum fees, there are no specific discounts available.

## CLOTHING SIZES

| Malta | UK | Rest of Europe | USA | |
|---|---|---|---|---|
| 46 | 36 | 46 | 36 | |
| 48 | 38 | 48 | 38 | |
| 50 | 40 | 50 | 40 | |
| 52 | 42 | 52 | 42 | Suits |
| 54 | 44 | 54 | 44 | |
| 56 | 46 | 56 | 46 | |
| 41 | 7 | 41 | 8 | |
| 42 | 7½ | 42 | 8½ | |
| 43 | 8½ | 43 | 9½ | |
| 44 | 9½ | 44 | 10½ | Shoes |
| 45 | 10½ | 45 | 11½ | |
| 46 | 11 | 46 | 12 | |
| 37 | 14½ | 37 | 14½ | |
| 38 | 15 | 38 | 15 | |
| 39/40 | 15½ | 39/40 | 15½ | |
| 41 | 16 | 41 | 16 | Shirts |
| 42 | 16½ | 42 | 16½ | |
| 43 | 17 | 43 | 17 | |
| 34 | 8 | 34 | 6 | |
| 36 | 10 | 36 | 8 | |
| 38 | 12 | 38 | 10 | |
| 40 | 14 | 40 | 12 | Dresses |
| 42 | 16 | 42 | 14 | |
| 44 | 18 | 44 | 16 | |
| 38 | 4½ | 38 | 6 | |
| 38 | 5 | 38 | 6½ | |
| 39 | 5½ | 39 | 7 | |
| 39 | 6 | 39 | 7½ | Shoes |
| 40 | 6½ | 40 | 8 | |
| 41 | 7 | 41 | 8½ | |

**WHEN DEPARTING**

● Contact the airport, airline or travel representative the day prior to leaving to ensure flights are unchanged.

● Arrive 90 minutes before your scheduled flight departure time (particularly during summer) or you may lose your flight.

● Departing visitors must complete an Embarkation Card (available at check-in area) to present at passport control.

## LANGUAGE

Maltese and English are the official languages of Malta and Gozo. Almost everyone speaks English but it is Maltese that is normally heard on the streets and that predominates in the media. Maltese comprises a vast element of words of Italian, French and English origin. The alphabet consists of 29 characters: a, b, ċ (as ch in 'church'), d, e, f, ġ (as g in 'George'), g, h, ħ (as h in 'house'), i, j, k, l, m, n, għ (a single letter and usually silent), o, p, q. r, s, t, u, v, w, x, ż (as z in 'zebra') and z. Menus are all in English but road signs are for the most part in Maltese. Below is a list of a few words that may be helpful.

| | | | |
|---|---|---|---|
| hotel | *lukanda* | breakfast | *l-ewwel ikla tal-jum* |
| room | *kamra* | toilet/bathroom | *kamra tal banju* |
| ...single/double | *singlu/doppja* | shower | *doċċa* |
| ...one/two nights | *lejl/żewġ iljieli* | balcony | *gallarija* |
| ...per person/per room | *kull persuna/kull kamra* | reception | *'reception'* |
| | | key | *ċavetta* |
| reservation | *riserva* | room service | *servizz fil-kamra* |
| rate | *rata* | chambermaid | *kamriera* |

| | | | |
|---|---|---|---|
| bank | *bank* | American dollar | *dollaru Amerikan* |
| exchange office | *uffiċju tal-kambju* | banknote | *karta tal-flus* |
| post office | *posta* | coin | *munita* |
| cashier | *kaxxier* | credit card | *karta ta' kredtu* |
| foreign exchange | *uffiċju tal-kambju* | cheque book | *'cheque book'* |
| foreign currency | *flus barranin* | exchange rate | *rata tal-kambju* |
| pound sterling | *lira sterlina* | commission charge | *senserija* |

| | | | |
|---|---|---|---|
| restaurant | *restorant* | Dinner | *ikla* |
| café | *café* | starter | *'starter'* |
| table | *mejda* | main course | *ikla* |
| menu | *menu* | dessert | *deserta* |
| set menu | *menu fiss* | drink | *xorb* |
| wine list | *lista ta' l-inbid* | waiter | *waiter* |
| lunch | *kolazjonn* | the bill | *kont* |

| | | | |
|---|---|---|---|
| aeroplane | *ajruplan* | ..single/return | *singlu/bir-ritorn* |
| airport | *ajruport* | ..first/second class | *l-ewwl/tieni klassi* |
| bus | *karozza tal-linja* | ticket office | *uffiċju tal biljetti* |
| ..station | *stazzjon tal karozza tal-linja* | timetable | *orarju* |
| | | seat | *seat/post* |
| station | *stazzjon tal ferrovija* | non-smoking | *tpejjipx* |
| ferry | *vapur* | reserved | *riservat* |
| ..terminal | *terminal* | | |
| | ticket | *biljett* | |

| | | | |
|---|---|---|---|
| yes | *iva* | help! | *ajjut!* |
| no | *le* | today | *illum* |
| please | *jekk jogħġbok* | tomorrow | *għada* |
| thank you | *grazzi* | yesterday | *il-bieraħ* |
| hello | *merħba* | how much? | *kemm?* |
| goodbye | *saħħa* | expensive | *għoli* |
| goodnight | *il-lejl it-tajjeb* | open | *miftuħ* |
| sorry | *jiddispjaċini* | closed | *magħluq* |

# INDEX

## Acknowledgements

The Automobile Association wishes to thank the following libraries, photographers and associations for their assistance in the preparation of this book: **MRI BANKERS' GUIDE TO FOREIGN CURRENCY** 119; **MUSEUM OF FINE ARTS VALETTA** 20; **ST AGATHA'S & ST PAUL'S CATACOMBS** 10, 15b, 24; **SPECTRUM COLOUR LIBRARY** 19, 46, 53.

The remaining pictures are from the Association's own library (**AA PHOTO LIBRARY**) with contributions from: **PHILIP ENTICNAP** 5b, 7, 8a, 9b, 12, 13, 15a, 16, 17, 18, 21, 22, 23, 26, 27b, 30, 31, 33, 39, 42, 54, 61, 64, 68c, 71, 76, 79, 80, 84, 86, 91a, 91b, 117a; **DAVID VINCENT** 27a; **WYN VOYSEY** 1, 2, 5a, 6, 8b, 9a, 11, 25, 36, 37, 38, 40, 43, 44, 45, 49, 50, 57, 59, 60, 63, 66, 67, 68a, 68b, 69a, 70, 72a, 72b, 74, 75, 81, 83, 87, 88, 89, 90, 117b, 122a, 122b, 122c.

## Authors' Acknowledgements

Pat Levy and Sean Sheehan would particularly like to thank Adriana Cacciottolo at the Malta Tourist Office in London. Thanks too, to the many people in Malta who helped with information for this edition; special thanks to the AA readers of the first edition who provided excellent feedback and suggestions. The Automobile Association wishes to thank Jeffrey Mizzi and Donald Pace for their assistance.

Updated by Lindsay Bennett

# *Dear Essential Traveller*

**Your comments, opinions and recommendations are very important to us. So please help us to improve our travel guides by taking a few minutes to complete this simple questionnaire.**

*You do not need a stamp (unless posted outside the UK). If you do not want to cut this page from your guide, then photocopy it or write your answers on a plain sheet of paper.*

*Send to*: **The Editor, AA World Travel Guides, FREEPOST SCE 4598, Basingstoke RG21 4GY.**

## Your recommendations...

We always encourage readers' recommendations for restaurants, nightlife or shopping – if your recommendation is used in the next edition of the guide, we will send you a *FREE* AA *Essential* **Guide** of your choice. Please state below the establishment name, location and your reasons for recommending it.

_____

_____

_____

_____

Please send me **AA *Essential*** _____

## About this guide...

Which title did you buy?
   AA *Essential* _____

Where did you buy it? _____

When? m m / y y

Why did you choose an AA *Essential* Guide? _____

_____

_____

_____

_____

Did this guide meet your expectations?
   Exceeded ☐   Met all ☐   Met most ☐   Fell below ☐

   Please give your reasons _____

_____

_____

_____

*continued on next page...*

Were there any aspects of this guide that you particularly liked? ________

________

________

Is there anything we could have done better? ________

________

________

## About you...

Name (*Mr/Mrs/Ms*) ________

Address ________

________

________ Postcode ________

Daytime tel nos ________

Please only give us your mobile phone number if you wish to hear from us about other products and services from the AA and partners by text or mms.

Which age group are you in?

Under 25 ☐ 25–34 ☐ 35–44 ☐ 45–54 ☐ 55–64 ☐ 65+ ☐

How many trips do you make a year?

Less than one ☐ One ☐ Two ☐ Three or more ☐

Are you an AA member? Yes ☐ No ☐

## About your trip...

When did you book? m m / y y When did you travel? m m / y y

How long did you stay? ________

Was it for business or leisure? ________

Did you buy any other travel guides for your trip?

If yes, which ones? ________

Thank you for taking the time to complete this questionnaire. Please send it to us as soon as possible, and remember, you do not need a stamp (*unless posted outside the UK*).

*Happy Holidays!*

The information we hold about you will be used to provide the products and services requested and for identification, account administration, analysis, and fraud/loss prevention purposes. More details about how that information is used is in our privacy statement, which you'll find under the heading "Personal Information" in our terms and conditions and on our website: www.theAA.com. Copies are also available from us by post, by contacting the Data Protection Manager at AA, Fanum House, Basing View, Basingstoke, Hampshire RG21 4EA.

We may want to contact you about other products and services provided by us, or our partners (by mail, telephone) but please tick the box if you DO NOT wish to hear about such products and services from us by mail or telephone. ☐